W9-BSH-691

HANDY SUBSTITUTIONS

INGREDIENT NEEDED	SUBSTITUTE
Baking Products	
1 cup self-rising flour	1 cup all-purpose flour, 1 teaspoon baking powder, and ½ teaspoon salt
1 cup cake flour	1 cup minus 2 tablespoons all-purpose flour
1 cup all-purpose flour	1 cup plus 2 tablespoons cake flour
1 cup powdered sugar	1 cup sugar and 1 tablespoon cornstarch (processed in food processor)
1 cup honey	1¼ cups sugar and ¼ cup water
1 teaspoon baking powder	¼ teaspoon baking soda and ½ teaspoon cream of tartar
1 tablespoon cornstarch	2 tablespoons all-purpose flour
1 tablespoon tapioca	1½ tablespoons all-purpose flour
½ cup chopped pecans	½ cup regular oats, toasted (in baked products)
1 ounce or square unsweetened chocolate	3 tablespoons cocoa and 1 tablespoon butter or margarine
Eggs and Dairy Products	
2 large eggs	3 small eggs
1 cup fat-free milk	½ cup evaporated fat-free milk and ½ cup water
1 cup plain yogurt	1 cup buttermilk
1 cup nonfat sour cream	1 cup nonfat yogurt and 1 tablespoon cornstarch (for cooking)
Vegetable Products	
1 pound fresh mushrooms, sliced	1 (8-ounce) can sliced mushrooms, drained, or 3 ounces dried
1 medium onion, chopped	1 tablespoon instant minced onion or 1 tablespoon onion powder
3 tablespoons chopped shallots	2½ tablespoons chopped onion and 1 teaspoon chopped garlic
Seasoning Products	
1 tablespoon chopped fresh herbs	1 teaspoon dried herbs or ¼ teaspoon powdered herbs
1 clove garlic	⅛ teaspoon garlic powder or minced dried garlic or 1 teaspoon bottled minced garlic
1 tablespoon dried orange peel	1½ teaspoons orange extract or 1 tablespoon grated fresh orange rind
1 teaspoon ground allspice	½ teaspoon ground cinnamon and ½ teaspoon ground cloves
1 teaspoon pumpkin pie spice	½ teaspoon ground cinnamon, ¼ teaspoon ground ginger, ⅛ teaspoon ground allspice, and ⅛ teaspoon ground nutmeg
Alcohol	
2 tablespoons amaretto	¼ to ½ teaspoon almond extract
2 tablespoons dry sherry or bourbon	1 to 2 teaspoons vanilla extract
¼ cup Marsala	¼ cup dry white wine and 1 teaspoon brandy
¼ cup or more white wine	Equal measure of apple juice (in sweet dishes) or reduced-sodium chicken broth (in savory dishes)
¼ cup or more red wine	Equal measure of red grape juice or cranberry juice

Buttermilk Biscuits
(recipe, page 31)

Southwestern Vegetable Soup
(recipe, page 165)

Jalapeño Cornbread
(recipe, page 30)

Mocha Fudge Pudding
(recipe, page 45)

Lemony Strawberry-
Spinach Salad
(recipe, page 130)

Weight Watchers®
Simple & Classic
Homecooking

Oxmoor House®

© 2000 by Oxmoor House, Inc.

Book Division of Southern Progress Corporation

P.O. Box 2463, Birmingham, Alabama 35201

All rights reserved. No part of this book may be reproduced in any form or by any means without the prior written permission of the publisher, excepting brief quotes in connection with reviews written specifically for inclusion in a magazine or newspaper.

LIBRARY OF CONGRESS CONTROL NUMBER: 00-132918

ISBN: 0-8487-1958-1

Printed in the United States of America

First Printing 2000

Be sure to check with your health-care provider before making any changes in your diet.

Weight Watchers is a registered trademark of Weight Watchers International, Inc., and is used under license by Healthy Living, Inc.

EDITOR-IN-CHIEF: Nancy Fitzpatrick Wyatt

SENIOR FOODS EDITOR: Katherine M. Eakin

SENIOR EDITOR, COPY AND HOMES: Olivia Kindig Wells

ART DIRECTOR: James Boone

Weight Watchers Simple & Classic Homecooking

EDITOR: Suzanne Henson, M.S., R.D.

ASSOCIATE ART DIRECTOR: Cynthia R. Cooper

DESIGNER: Clare T. Minges

COPY EDITORS: Jacqueline Giovanelli, Shari K. Wimberly

EDITORIAL ASSISTANT: Suzanne Powell

DIRECTOR, TEST KITCHENS: Elizabeth Tyler Luckett

ASSISTANT DIRECTOR, TEST KITCHENS: Julie Christopher

RECIPE EDITOR: Gayle Hays Sadler

TEST KITCHENS STAFF: Gretchen Feldtman, R.D.; Natalie E. King; Rebecca Mohr Boggan; Jan A. Smith

SENIOR PHOTOGRAPHERS: Jim Bathie, John O'Hagan

SENIOR PHOTO STYLIST: Kay E. Clarke

PHOTOGRAPHER: Brit Huckabay

PHOTO STYLIST: Virginia R. Cravens

PUBLISHING SYSTEMS ADMINISTRATOR: Rick Tucker

DIRECTOR, PRODUCTION AND DISTRIBUTION: Phillip Lee

ASSOCIATE PRODUCTION MANAGER: Vanessa Cobbs Richardson

PRODUCTION ASSISTANT: Faye Porter Bonner

CONTRIBUTORS:

COPY EDITOR: Jan Hanby

RECIPE DEVELOPMENT: Patti A. Bess; Lorrie Hulston; Carol H. Munson; OTT Communications; Marcia K. Stanley, M.S., R.D.

TEST KITCHENS: Leigh Mullinax; Kathleen Royal Phillips; Kate M. Wheeler, R.D.

COVER: Classic Hamburger, page 84; Cheese Fries, page 178

BACK COVER: Chocolate Cream Pie, page 48

WE'RE HERE FOR YOU!

We at Oxmoor House are dedicated to serving you with reliable information that expands your imagination and enriches your life. We welcome your comments and suggestions. Please write us at:

Oxmoor House, Inc.

Editor, *Weight Watchers Simple & Classic Homecooking*

2100 Lakeshore Drive

Birmingham, AL 35209

To order additional publications, call 1-205-877-6560.

Contents

Seven Secrets of
Healthier Homecooking

Do you crave the foods you grew up with, but don't want all the fat and calories of those traditional recipes? Well, we've found ways to lighten your favorites without sacrificing flavor.

On the following page, we've shared our secrets for lightening the ever-popular Creamy Chicken Casserole. A before and after comparison shows what a difference a few simple changes can make.

We cut the fat and calorie content of the original recipe and kept an eye on both sodium and cholesterol without losing its rich taste and creamy texture.

Enjoy this lightened recipe and others in this cookbook. We've done the work for you. Then, use our seven secrets of healthier homecooking to lighten some of your family's favorites.

1. SHOP AROUND: Today's products have caught up with consumers' desire to enjoy low-fat foods that taste good. Substitute low-fat soups, sour cream, and other convenience products for their heavy alternatives.

2. BEEF TIPS: If a recipe calls for ground beef, substitute ground round, the leanest type of ground beef. Brown the meat in a nonstick skillet, and then drain it in a paper towel-lined colander. Use paper towels to wipe the skillet dry to eliminate even more fat before returning the meat to the skillet. Choose whole cuts of beef with the least amount of marbling (flecks of fat within the lean part of the meat). Trim all visible fat before cooking.

3. SPRAY AWAY: Cooking spray is a healthy alternative to butter, margarine, vegetable shortening, and oil when coating skillets and baking dishes. It also makes cleanup a breeze.

4. CHEESE, PLEASE: Switch to higher-flavored, full-bodied cheeses like reduced-fat sharp Cheddar cheese. When you use a sharp-flavored cheese, you get more flavor with less cheese.

5. STOCK UP: Keep chopped, cooked chicken breasts in the freezer so that you can easily put together entrées. Buy pre-cooked chicken, available in your super-market's frozen food aisle, or a rotisserie chicken when you need a quick meal.

6. SAUCE SAVVY: Fat-free half-and-half, low-fat sour cream, or evaporated fat-free milk makes a creamy replacement for regular half-and-half and whipping cream in many sauce recipes.

7. GO NUTS: Toasting nuts before adding them to a recipe stretches their flavor without adding fat. Try chopping them a little finer than normal so that you get nutty flavor in every bite.

Before Creamy Chicken Casserole

1   (10.75-ounce) can **cream of chicken soup,** undiluted
1   (8-ounce) carton **sour cream**
1   tablespoon poppy seeds
3   cups chopped cooked **chicken**
1½ cups crushed **round buttery crackers** (about 40 crackers)
½   cup **butter or margarine,** melted

1. Combine first 4 ingredients; spoon into a **lightly greased** 11-x 7-inch baking dish. Combine crushed crackers and butter, and sprinkle over chicken mixture. Bake, uncovered, at 350° for 30 minutes. Yield: 4 (1-cup) servings.

BEFORE & AFTER	
Serving Size	
1 cup	1 cup
POINTS	
17	6
Calories	
690	270
Fat	
46.0g	10.5g
Sodium	
1067mg	520mg
Cholesterol	
166mg	83mg

After Creamy Poppy Seed Chicken Casserole

1   (10.75-ounce) can **reduced-fat, reduced-sodium cream of chicken soup,** undiluted
1   (8-ounce) carton **66%-less-fat sour cream**
1   tablespoon poppy seeds
2   cups chopped cooked **chicken breast**
Cooking spray
15 reduced-fat **round buttery crackers,** crushed
1½ tablespoons **reduced-calorie margarine,** melted

1. Combine soup, sour cream, and poppy seeds; stir well. Add chicken. Pour mixture into a 2-quart baking dish **coated with cooking spray**. Combine crushed crackers and margarine; sprinkle over chicken mixture. Bake at 350° for 30 minutes. Yield: 4 (1-cup) servings.

POINTS: 6   **EXCHANGES:** 1 Starch, 3 Lean Meat   **PER SERVING:** Calories 270, Carbohydrate 14.1g, Fat 10.5g (saturated 3.9g), Fiber 0.2g, Protein 26.9g, Cholesterol 83mg, Sodium 520mg, Calcium 163mg, Iron 1.0mg

How we lightened it

• Used reduced-fat, reduced-sodium cream of chicken soup.
• Substituted low-fat sour cream for regular sour cream.
• Used chicken breast instead of a mix of white and dark meat.

• Switched to reduced-fat buttery crackers and reduced the number used.
• Substituted reduced-calorie margarine for regular margarine and reduced the amount.
• Coated the baking dish with cooking spray instead of vegetable shortening.

About These Recipes

Weight Watchers® *Simple & Classic Homecooking* gives you the
nutrition facts you want to know. To make your life easier, we've provided
the following useful information with every recipe:

- A number calculated through *POINTS*® Food System, an integral part of Weight
  Watchers *1•2•3 Success*® Weight Loss Plan
- Diabetic exchange values for those who use them as a guide for planning meals
- A complete nutrient analysis per serving

POINTS Food System

Every recipe in the book includes a
number assigned through *POINTS* value.
This system uses a formula based on the
calorie, fat, and fiber content of the food.
Foods with more calories and fat (like
a slice of pepperoni pizza) receive high
numbers, while fruits and vegetables receive
low numbers. For more information about
the *1•2•3 Success* Weight Loss Plan and
the Weight Watchers meeting nearest you,
call 1-800-651-6000.

Diabetic Exchanges

Exchange values are provided for people
who use them for calorie-controlled diets
and for people with diabetes. All foods
within a certain group contain approximately
the same amount of nutrients and calories,
so one serving of a food from a food group
can be substituted or exchanged for one
serving of any other item on the list. The
food groups are meat, starch, vegetable,
fruit, fat, and milk. The exchange values are
based on the *Exchange Lists for Meal*

Planning developed by the American
Diabetes Association and the American
Dietetic Association.

Nutritional Analyses

Each recipe has a complete list of nutrients;
numbers are based on these assumptions:

- Unless otherwise indicated, meat, poultry, and fish refer to skinned, boned, and
  cooked servings.
- When we give a range for an ingredient
  (3 to 3½ cups flour, for instance), we
  calculate using the lesser amount.
- Some alcohol calories evaporate during
  heating; the analysis reflects that.
- Only the amount of marinade absorbed
  by the food is used in calculation.
- Garnishes and optional ingredients are
  not included in analysis.

The nutritional values used in our calcula-
tions either come from a computer program
by Computrition, Inc., or are provided by
food manufacturers.

beverages
&
snacks

Mint Limeade

POINTS:

2

EXCHANGES:

1½ Starch

PER SERVING:

Calories 92
Carbohydrate 24.3g
Fat 0.0g (saturated 0.0g)
Fiber 0.0g
Protein 0.1g
Cholesterol 0mg
Sodium 2mg
Calcium 2mg
Iron 0.3mg

2   cups boiling water
2   mint tea bags
1   (12-ounce) can frozen limeade concentrate, thawed

1. Combine water and tea bags in a 2-cup glass measure; cover and steep 7 minutes. Remove and discard tea bags. Cool to room temperature.

2. Combine limeade and 2 cans of water in a 2-quart pitcher; add tea, stirring well. Cover and chill. Serve over crushed ice, if desired. Yield: 7 (1-cup) servings.

COOKING SECRET: Enhance the flavor of this summertime treat by serving it with citrus-mint ice cubes. Simply place a small mint sprig and a lime slice in each section of ice cube trays; add sugar-free lemon-lime soft drink. Freeze until firm.

Strawberry Smoothie (photo, page 22)

1½ cups halved fresh strawberries
1 (8-ounce) carton strawberry-banana reduced-fat yogurt
½ cup peeled, cubed mango
⅓ cup pineapple juice
2 tablespoons honey
Ice cubes
4 whole strawberries

1. Combine first 5 ingredients in container of an electric blender. Cover and process until smooth, stopping once to scrape down sides.

2. Add enough ice cubes to bring mixture to 5-cup level; process until smooth.

3. Pour into glasses to serve. Garnish with whole strawberries. Serve immediately. Yield: 4 (1¼-cup) servings.

> **COOKING SECRET:** If mango is not available, substitute half of a banana or increase the strawberries to 2 cups.

POINTS:
2

EXCHANGES:
1 Starch
1 Fruit

PER SERVING:
Calories 140
Carbohydrate 31.8g
Fat 1.0g (saturated 0.4g)
Fiber 2.4g
Protein 3.0g
Cholesterol 2mg
Sodium 32mg
Calcium 97mg
Iron 0.5mg

Candy Apple Cider

POINTS:

3

EXCHANGES:

½ Starch

2 Fruit

PER SERVING:

Calories 156

Carbohydrate 39.4g

Fat 0.2g (saturated 0.0g)

Fiber 0.5g

Protein 0.1g

Cholesterol 0mg

Sodium 11mg

Calcium 18mg

Iron 0.9mg

4   cups apple cider
2   tablespoons red cinnamon candies
1   (1-inch) piece peeled gingerroot
4   (3-inch) sticks cinnamon (optional)

1. Combine first 3 ingredients in a medium saucepan. Bring mixture to a boil; reduce heat and simmer, stirring constantly, until candy melts. Remove and discard gingerroot.

2. Pour into individual mugs to serve. Garnish with a cinnamon stick, if desired. Serve immediately. Yield: 4 (1-cup) servings.

COOKING SECRET: When buying fresh ginger, look for a smooth skin (wrinkled skin indicates that the root is dry and past its prime). It should have a fresh, spicy fragrance.

Creamy Hot Cocoa Mix

1   (15-ounce) package instant chocolate milk mix
1   (11-ounce) jar powdered nondairy coffee creamer
1⅓ cups sifted powdered sugar
1   (9.6-ounce) package instant nonfat dry milk powder
1   cup unsweetened cocoa

1. Combine all ingredients in a large bowl; store in an airtight container in a cool place. Yield: 10⅓ cups (⅓ cup per serving).

HOT CHOCOLATE BY THE CUP		
NUMBER OF 1-CUP SERVINGS	**HOT COCOA MIX**	**BOILING WATER**
1	⅓ cup	1 cup
2	⅔ cup	2 cups
4	1⅓ cups	4 cups

POINTS:
4

EXCHANGES:
2 Starch
½ Fat

PER SERVING:
Calories 168
Carbohydrate 27.5g
Fat 3.2g (saturated 3.0g)
Fiber 0.6g
Protein 4.6g
Cholesterol 11mg
Sodium 285mg
Calcium 679mg
Iron 3.0mg

Guacamole

POINTS:

0

EXCHANGE:

Free

(up to 2 tablespoons)

PER SERVING:

Calories 17

Carbohydrate 1.4g

Fat 1.2g (saturated 0.2g)

Fiber 0.5g

Protein 0.6g

Cholesterol 0mg

Sodium 120mg

Calcium 8mg

Iron 0.4mg

1   cup cubed, peeled avocado (about 1 medium)
6   ounces firm, silken-style tofu, drained and cubed
1   (4.5-ounce) can diced green chiles, drained
½   cup chopped green onions
¼   cup nonfat mayonnaise
2   tablespoons chopped fresh parsley
2   tablespoons chopped fresh cilantro
3   to 4 tablespoons fresh lime juice
¾   teaspoon salt
2   cloves garlic, halved
1   jalapeño pepper, seeded

1. Position knife blade in food processor bowl; add all ingredients.

2. Process until smooth, scraping down sides if necessary. Spoon mixture into a bowl; cover and chill. Yield: 2 cups (1 tablespoon per serving).

COOKING SECRET: Fresh lime juice gives this guacamole a tart flavor. For added pizzazz, decrease the lime juice to 1 to 2 tablespoons and add a few drops of hot sauce. Serve this classic dip with baked tortilla chips.

Hummus

1   (15-ounce) can chickpeas (garbanzo beans)
3   tablespoons lemon juice
2   tablespoons chopped green onions
1   tablespoon tahini (sesame seed paste)
½   teaspoon salt
¼   teaspoon hot sauce
1   to 2 cloves garlic, minced

1. Drain beans, reserving ¼ cup liquid.

2. Combine beans, reserved liquid, and remaining ingredients in container of an electric blender. Cover and process until smooth. Cover and chill. Yield: 1 cup (1 tablespoon per serving).

COOKING SECRET: Try a flavor variation of this tasty Middle Eastern spread by adding ½ cup bottled roasted red peppers, drained and chopped, to the bean mixture before processing. This traditional puree of garbanzo beans and garlic is great as a dip with pita wedges or baked tortilla chips.

POINTS:
0

EXCHANGE:
½ Starch

PER SERVING:
Calories 32
Carbohydrate 5.4g
Fat 0.7g (saturated 0.1g)
Fiber 1.5g
Protein 1.2g
Cholesterol 0mg
Sodium 138mg
Calcium 12mg
Iron 0.4mg

Classic Onion Dip

POINTS:

0

EXCHANGE:

Free

(up to 3 tablespoons)

PER SERVING:

Calories 12

Carbohydrate 1.4g

Fat 0.0g (saturated 0.0g)

Fiber 0.1g

Protein 1.1g

Cholesterol 0mg

Sodium 40mg

Calcium 21mg

Iron 0.0mg

1   (8-ounce) carton nonfat sour cream
½   cup finely chopped onion
2   teaspoons low-sodium soy sauce
¼   teaspoon garlic pepper

1. Combine all ingredients in a medium bowl; stir well. Cover and chill 1 hour. Yield: 1 cup (1 tablespoon per serving).

TIP: Serve this dip with assorted raw fresh vegetables, Melba toast rounds, or reduced-fat crackers for a healthy snack.

Fresh Tomato Salsa

3 cups tomato, seeded and diced (about 3 large)
½ cup diced purple onion
3 tablespoons chopped fresh cilantro
3 tablespoons fresh lime juice
½ teaspoon salt
2 cloves garlic, minced
1 jalapeño pepper, seeded and diced

1. Combine all ingredients in a medium bowl. Let stand 30 minutes before serving. Yield: 2 cups (1 tablespoon per serving).

COOKING SECRET: Seeding the tomatoes prevents the salsa from being watery. To seed a tomato, cut it in half horizontally and scoop out the seeds with a spoon.

POINTS:
0

EXCHANGE:
Free

PER SERVING:
Calories 4
Carbohydrate 0.9g
Fat 0.0g (saturated 0.0g)
Fiber 0.2g
Protein 0.2g
Cholesterol 0mg
Sodium 38mg
Calcium 2mg
Iron 0.1mg

Sausage-Cheese Balls

POINTS:

1

EXCHANGES:

½ Starch

½ Fat

PER SERVING:

Calories 61

Carbohydrate 4.5g

Fat 3.3g (saturated 0.6g)

Fiber 0.2g

Protein 3.3g

Cholesterol 11mg

Sodium 180mg

Calcium 54mg

Iron 0.4mg

½ pound turkey breakfast sausage

1 cup (4 ounces) shredded reduced-fat sharp Cheddar cheese

3 tablespoons chopped fresh parsley

¼ teaspoon ground red pepper

1¼ cups reduced-fat biscuit and baking mix (such as Bisquick)

Cooking spray

1. Combine sausage, cheese, parsley, and pepper in a medium bowl, stirring well. Add biscuit and baking mix, and mix well.

2. Coat a baking sheet with cooking spray. Shape meat mixture into 1-inch balls; place balls on baking sheet and lightly coat with cooking spray.

3. Bake at 350° for 20 to 25 minutes or until done. Serve warm. Yield: 24 servings (1 sausage-cheese ball per serving).

TIP: If you are serving these appetizer favorites at a party, put them in a 1- or 2-quart slow cooker so that they stay warm throughout your gathering.

Caramel Corn Crunch
(recipe, page 27)

Strawberry Smoothie
(recipe, page 13)

Buttermilk-Cherry
Scones
(recipe, page 32)

23

Oatmeal-Molasses Bread
(recipe, page 38)

Chicken and Green Chile Quesadillas

6	(8-inch) flour tortillas
¾	cup low-fat roasted garlic-flavored cream cheese
2	skinned, boned roasted chicken breast halves, thinly sliced (such as Tyson)
2	(4.5-ounce) cans diced green chiles, drained
⅓	cup finely chopped purple onion
Cooking spray	

1. Spread each tortilla with 2 tablespoons cream cheese. Top evenly with chicken, chiles, and onion. Fold tortillas in half.

2. Coat a large skillet with cooking spray; place over medium heat until hot. Add tortillas, two at a time, and cook 1 minute on each side or until golden. Serve warm. Yield: 12 servings (one-half quesadilla per serving).

TIP: Serve these creamy quesadillas with Guacamole (page 16) and Fresh Tomato Salsa (page 19).

POINTS:
3

EXCHANGES:
1 Starch
1 Medium-Fat Meat

PER SERVING:
Calories 134
Carbohydrate 14.0g
Fat 4.5g (saturated 2.2g)
Fiber 0.9g
Protein 9.2g
Cholesterol 21mg
Sodium 514mg
Calcium 44mg
Iron 0.8mg

Deviled Eggs

POINTS:
1

EXCHANGE:
½ Medium-Fat Meat

PER SERVING:
Calories 39
Carbohydrate 1.1g
Fat 2.6g (saturated 0.5g)
Fiber 0.0g
Protein 2.7g
Cholesterol 74mg
Sodium 90mg
Calcium 10mg
Iron 0.2mg

6   hard-cooked eggs, peeled
2½ tablespoons reduced-fat mayonnaise
1   tablespoon sweet pickle relish, drained
1   tablespoon grated onion
1   teaspoon prepared mustard
⅛   teaspoon salt
Dash of ground white pepper
Paprika

1. Slice eggs in half lengthwise. Scoop out yolks, and place 4 yolks in a small bowl. (Reserve remaining yolks for another use.) Set whites aside.

2. Mash yolks with a fork. Add mayonnaise, pickle relish, onion, mustard, salt, and pepper; stir well.

3. Spoon mixture evenly into egg whites; sprinkle with paprika. Yield: 12 servings (1 egg half per serving).

COOKING SECRET: For perfect hard-cooked eggs, place eggs in a single layer in a saucepan. Add enough cold water to measure at least 1 inch above eggs. Cover and quickly bring to a boil. Remove from heat. Let stand, covered, in hot water 15 minutes for large eggs. Pour off water. Immediately run cold water over eggs or place them in ice water until completely cooled.

Caramel Corn Crunch (photo, page 21)

1 (3-ounce) package reduced-fat microwave popcorn (such as Orville Redenbacher's Smart Pop)
⅔ cup firmly packed brown sugar
¼ cup plus 2 tablespoons reduced-calorie margarine
¼ cup plus 2 tablespoons reduced-calorie maple-flavored syrup
1 teaspoon vanilla extract
¼ teaspoon baking soda
Cooking spray

1. Cook popcorn according to package directions. Place popped corn in a large bowl; set aside.

2. Combine sugar, margarine, and syrup in a 2-quart saucepan; place over medium heat. Bring to a boil, stirring constantly. Cook 5 minutes, without stirring, or until candy thermometer registers 250°. Remove from heat, and stir in vanilla and baking soda.

3. Pour syrup mixture over popcorn; stir until evenly coated.

4. Spread mixture onto 2 jelly-roll pans coated with cooking spray. Bake at 250° for 20 to 25 minutes or until mixture is crisp. Cool in pans on wire racks; break into small pieces. Store in an airtight container. Yield: 14 (1-cup) servings.

 TIP: Line the jelly-roll pans with aluminum foil, and coat the foil with cooking spray.

POINTS:
2

EXCHANGES:
1 Starch
½ Fat

PER SERVING:
Calories 89
Carbohydrate 15.8g
Fat 3.2g (saturated 0.4g)
Fiber 0.0g
Protein 0.8g
Cholesterol 0mg
Sodium 123mg
Calcium 9mg
Iron 0.2mg

Maple and Peanut Butter Granola

POINTS:

3

EXCHANGES:

1½ Starch

½ Fat

PER SERVING:

Calories 141

Carbohydrate 26.8g

Fat 2.7g (saturated 0.5g)

Fiber 2.1g

Protein 3.7g

Cholesterol 0mg

Sodium 90mg

Calcium 23mg

Iron 1.1mg

3   tablespoons crunchy reduced-fat peanut butter
½   cup pure maple syrup
3   tablespoons water
1   teaspoon ground cinnamon
¼   teaspoon salt
3   cups regular or quick-cooking oats
Cooking spray
½   cup golden raisins

1. Combine first 5 ingredients in a small saucepan; stir well with a wire whisk. Bring to a boil; reduce heat, and simmer 1 minute.

2. Pour hot mixture over oats; stir well to coat oat mixture. Spread on a baking sheet coated with cooking spray. Bake at 300° for 15 minutes. Reduce heat to 250°; bake 15 minutes.

3. Add raisins, and stir well. Bake an additional 15 minutes. Turn oven off, and allow to cool in oven 20 to 30 minutes. Yield: 11 servings (⅓ cup per serving).

 TIP: Stir some granola into 8 ounces low-fat vanilla yogurt for a quick but hearty breakfast.

breads

Cornbread (photo, page 2)

POINTS:

3

EXCHANGES:

2 Starch

PER SERVING:

Calories 145

Carbohydrate 28.6g

Fat 1.6g (saturated 0.4g)

Fiber 2.6g

Protein 4.6g

Cholesterol 25mg

Sodium 367mg

Calcium 99mg

Iron 1.4mg

1¼ cups yellow cornmeal
¾   cup all-purpose flour
2   teaspoons baking powder
½   teaspoon baking soda
¼   teaspoon salt
1   tablespoon sugar
1   cup low-fat buttermilk
1   (8.5-ounce) can cream-style corn
1   egg, lightly beaten
Cooking spray

1. Combine first 6 ingredients in a medium bowl; stir well.

2. Combine buttermilk, corn, and egg in a small bowl; stir well.
Add to cornmeal mixture, stirring just until dry ingredients are
moistened. Pour batter into an 8-inch square baking pan coated
with cooking spray.

3. Bake at 425° for 20 to 22 minutes or until golden. Cool 5
minutes in pan on a wire rack. Remove from pan and cut into
squares. Serve warm. Yield: 9 servings (1 square per serving).

COOKING SECRET: For a spicy flavor option, add 3 tablespoons minced jalapeño pepper (about 3 small peppers)
and ½ cup sliced green onions to the batter. Serve with
Southwestern Vegetable Soup (page 165).

Buttermilk Biscuits (photo, page 1)

2 cups all-purpose flour

2½ teaspoons baking powder

¼ teaspoon baking soda

¼ teaspoon salt

2 teaspoons sugar

3 tablespoons chilled reduced-calorie stick margarine, cut into small pieces

¾ cup low-fat buttermilk

Butter-flavored cooking spray (such as I Can't Believe It's Not Butter)

Reduced-calorie jelly (optional)

1. Combine first 5 ingredients in a medium bowl; cut in margarine with pastry blender until mixture resembles coarse meal. Add buttermilk, stirring just until dry ingredients are moistened.

2. Turn dough out onto a lightly floured surface, and knead 10 to 12 times. Roll dough to ½-inch thickness; cut into rounds with a 2-inch biscuit cutter.

3. Place rounds on an ungreased baking sheet. Bake at 425° for 10 to 12 minutes or until golden. Lightly spray biscuits with cooking spray. Serve with reduced-calorie jelly, if desired. Yield: 16 biscuits (1 biscuit per serving).

> **COOKING SECRET:** Handle dough with a light touch for fluffy biscuits. Biscuit dough should be slightly sticky and should be kneaded gently. Take care to keep the cutter straight as you cut the dough; the biscuits will rise evenly if you do.

POINTS:

2

EXCHANGE:

1 Starch

PER SERVING:

Calories 75

Carbohydrate 13.2g

Fat 1.6g (saturated 0.1g)

Fiber 0.4g

Protein 2.0g

Cholesterol 0mg

Sodium 167mg

Calcium 59mg

Iron 0.8mg

Buttermilk-Cherry Scones (photo, page 23)

POINTS:
4

EXCHANGES:
2 Starch
1 Fat

PER SERVING:
Calories 173
Carbohydrate 28.4g
Fat 4.5g (saturated 1.0g)
Fiber 0.9g
Protein 4.1g
Cholesterol 19mg
Sodium 239mg
Calcium 69mg
Iron 1.2mg

2 cups all-purpose flour
1½ teaspoons baking powder
½ teaspoon baking soda
¼ teaspoon salt
¼ cup sugar
¼ cup chilled stick margarine, cut into small pieces
⅔ cup dried tart cherries
1 egg, lightly beaten
½ cup low-fat buttermilk
Cooking spray
1 egg white, lightly beaten
1 tablespoon sugar

1. Combine first 5 ingredients in a bowl; cut in margarine with a pastry blender until mixture resembles coarse meal. Add cherries; toss well. Combine egg and buttermilk; add to dry ingredients, stirring just until moistened. (Dough will be sticky.)

2. Turn dough out onto a lightly floured surface; with floured hands, knead 4 or 5 times. Pat dough into an 8-inch circle on a baking sheet coated with cooking spray. Cut into 12 wedges, cutting to but not through bottom of dough. Brush with egg white, and sprinkle with 1 tablespoon sugar. Bake at 400° for 15 minutes or until golden. Serve hot. Yield: 12 scones (1 scone per serving).

 TIP: Substitute ⅓ cup chopped dried apricots for the dried cherries for a flavor variation.

Lemon-Poppy Seed Muffins

1¼ cups unprocessed oat bran
¾   cup all-purpose flour
1   teaspoon baking powder
½   teaspoon baking soda
½   cup sugar
1   tablespoon grated lemon rind
2   teaspoons poppy seeds
1   (8-ounce) carton lemon nonfat yogurt
½   cup low-fat buttermilk
¼   cup fat-free egg substitute
2   tablespoons vegetable oil
½   teaspoon vanilla extract
¼   teaspoon lemon extract
Cooking spray
⅓   cup sifted powdered sugar
1   tablespoon fresh lemon juice

POINTS:

3

EXCHANGES:
1½ Starch
½ Fat

PER SERVING:
Calories 152
Carbohydrate 25.9g
Fat 3.5g (saturated 0.6g)
Fiber 1.5g
Protein 4.5g
Cholesterol 1mg
Sodium 135mg
Calcium 94mg
Iron 1.1mg

1. Combine first 7 ingredients in a bowl; make a well in center of mixture. Combine yogurt and next 5 ingredients, stirring well; add to dry ingredients, stirring just until dry ingredients are moistened.

2. Spoon batter into muffin pans coated with cooking spray, filling three-fourths full. Bake at 400° for 20 to 22 minutes or until lightly browned. Remove muffins from pans; place on a wire rack.

3. Combine powdered sugar and lemon juice, stirring mixture well; drizzle over warm muffins. Yield: 12 muffins (1 muffin per serving).

 TIP: One large lemon should give you enough rind and juice for this recipe.

Molasses-Bran Muffins

POINTS:
2

EXCHANGES:
1½ Starch

PER SERVING:
Calories 124
Carbohydrate 26.4g
Fat 1.8g (saturated 0.3g)
Fiber 3.4g
Protein 3.1g
Cholesterol 0mg
Sodium 128mg
Calcium 105mg
Iron 2.3mg

1¼ cups unprocessed wheat bran
1 cup all-purpose flour
2 teaspoons baking powder
¼ teaspoon baking soda
½ teaspoon ground cinnamon
¾ cup unsweetened applesauce
½ cup fat-free milk
⅓ cup dark molasses
¼ cup fat-free egg substitute
1 tablespoon vegetable oil
½ cup raisins
Cooking spray

1. Combine first 5 ingredients in a bowl; make a well in center of mixture. Combine applesauce and next 4 ingredients; add to dry ingredients, stirring just until moistened. Stir in raisins.

2. Spoon batter into muffin pans coated with cooking spray, filling two-thirds full. Bake at 400° for 18 to 20 minutes or until golden. Remove from pans immediately, and place on a wire rack. Yield: 12 muffins (1 muffin per serving).

 COOKING SECRET: Dark molasses gives these muffins a wonderful flavor similar to gingerbread.

Blueberry Pancakes

1   cup all-purpose flour
2   teaspoons baking powder
¼   teaspoon baking soda
¼   teaspoon salt
1   tablespoon sugar
1⅓ cups low-fat buttermilk
¼   cup fat-free egg substitute
1   tablespoon vegetable oil
½   cup frozen blueberries
Cooking spray

1. Combine first 5 ingredients in a large bowl. Combine buttermilk, egg substitute, and oil; add to dry ingredients, stirring just until dry ingredients are moistened. Stir in blueberries.

2. For each pancake, pour ¼ cup batter onto a hot griddle or skillet coated with cooking spray. Cook until tops are bubbly and edges look cooked; turn and cook other sides. Yield: 12 pancakes (2 pancakes per serving).

COOKING SECRET: Watch the surface of the pancake as it's cooking. When the top is full of bubbles, it's time to flip the pancake.

POINTS:
3

EXCHANGES:
1½ Starch
½ Fat

PER SERVING:
Calories 143
Carbohydrate 23.6g
Fat 2.9g (saturated 0.6g)
Fiber 0.9g
Protein 5.8g
Cholesterol 2mg
Sodium 402mg
Calcium 181mg
Iron 1.4mg

Banana Bread

POINTS:
4

EXCHANGES:
2 Starch
1 Fat

PER SERVING:
Calories 187
Carbohydrate 31.5g
Fat 5.5g (saturated 1.0g)
Fiber 1.2g
Protein 3.6g
Cholesterol 19mg
Sodium 199mg
Calcium 78mg
Iron 1.4mg

2   cups all-purpose flour
2   teaspoons baking powder
½   teaspoon baking soda
¼   teaspoon salt
½   teaspoon ground cinnamon
½   cup firmly packed brown sugar
1   cup mashed ripe banana (about 2 medium)
½   cup vanilla low-fat yogurt
3   tablespoons vegetable oil
1   egg, lightly beaten
Cooking spray
3   tablespoons chopped pecans, toasted

1. Combine first 6 ingredients in a medium bowl; make a well in center of mixture. Combine banana, yogurt, oil, and egg; add mixture to dry ingredients, stirring just until moistened.

2. Spoon batter into a 9- x 5-inch loafpan coated with cooking spray. Sprinkle pecans over batter. Bake at 350° for 45 to 55 minutes or until a wooden pick inserted in center comes out clean. Let cool in pan 10 minutes on a wire rack; remove from pan, and let cool on a wire rack. Yield: 12 slices (1 slice per serving).

COOKING SECRET: When banana peels turn black, the banana is ripe, extra sweet, and ideal for making banana bread or muffins.

Classic White Bread

1   cup fat-free milk
2   teaspoons vegetable oil
1½ teaspoons sugar
1   teaspoon salt
3¼ cups all-purpose flour
1   package active dry yeast
Cooking spray

1. Combine milk, oil, sugar, and salt in a small saucepan; heat until very warm, stirring occasionally. Cool to 120° to 130°.

2. Combine flour and yeast in a large mixing bowl; stir well. Gradually add milk mixture to flour mixture, beating well at low speed of a heavy-duty stand mixer. Beat 2 additional minutes at medium speed.

3. Turn dough out onto a lightly floured surface, and knead until smooth and elastic (about 6 to 8 minutes). Place in a large bowl coated with cooking spray, turning to coat top. Cover and let rise in a warm place (85°), free from drafts, 1 hour or until doubled in bulk.

4. Punch dough down; turn out onto a lightly floured surface and knead lightly 4 or 5 times. Roll dough into a 10- x 6-inch rectangle. Roll up dough, starting at short side, pressing firmly to eliminate air pockets; pinch ends to seal.

5. Place dough, seam side down, in an 8½- x 4½-inch loafpan coated with cooking spray. Cover and let rise in a warm place, free from drafts, 45 minutes or until doubled in bulk.

6. Bake at 375° for 25 minutes or until loaf sounds hollow when tapped. Remove bread from pan immediately; let cool on a wire rack. Yield: 16 slices (1 slice per serving).

POINTS:

2

EXCHANGES:

1½ Starch

PER SERVING:

Calories 106
Carbohydrate 20.6g
Fat 0.9g (saturated 0.2g)
Fiber 0.8g
Protein 3.3g
Cholesterol 0mg
Sodium 155mg
Calcium 22mg
Iron 1.3mg

Oatmeal-Molasses Bread (photo, page 24)

POINTS:

3

EXCHANGES:

2 Starch

½ Fat

PER SERVING:

Calories 158

Carbohydrate 29.1g

Fat 2.6g (saturated 0.5g)

Fiber 1.4g

Protein 4.3g

Cholesterol 0mg

Sodium 131mg

Calcium 40mg

Iron 1.9mg

¾ cup fat-free milk
¼ cup molasses
2 tablespoons stick margarine
2½ to 2¾ cups all-purpose flour, divided
1 package rapid-rise yeast
½ teaspoon salt
¾ cup quick-cooking oats
Cooking spray
1 tablespoon quick-cooking oats

1. Combine milk, molasses, and margarine in a small saucepan; heat until margarine melts, stirring occasionally. Cool to 120° to 130°.

2. Combine 1 cup flour, yeast, and salt in a large mixing bowl; stir well. Gradually add milk mixture to flour mixture, beating well at low speed of a heavy-duty stand mixer. Beat 3 additional minutes at medium speed. Gradually stir in ¾ cup oats and enough remaining flour to make a soft dough.

3. Turn dough out onto a lightly floured surface, and knead until smooth and elastic (about 5 minutes). Place in a large bowl coated with cooking spray, turning to coat top. Cover and let rise in a warm place (85°), free from drafts, 40 minutes or until doubled in bulk.

4. Punch dough down; let rest 10 minutes. Shape dough into a 6-inch diameter ball and flatten slightly; place on a baking sheet coated with cooking spray. Cover and let rise in a warm place, free from drafts, 30 minutes or until doubled in bulk.

5. Coat top of loaf with cooking spray; sprinkle with 1 table-spoon oats. Bake at 375° for 26 to 28 minutes or until loaf sounds hollow when tapped. Remove bread from baking sheet immediately; let cool on a wire rack. Yield: 12 wedges (1 wedge per serving).

desserts

Tropical Banana Pudding

POINTS:

4

EXCHANGES:

3 Starch

½ Fat

PER SERVING:

Calories 218

Carbohydrate 43.7g

Fat 2.1g (saturated 0.9g)

Fiber 1.0g

Protein 4.3g

Cholesterol 2mg

Sodium 141mg

Calcium 88mg

Iron 0.8mg

½   cup sugar
¼   cup cornstarch
⅛   teaspoon salt
2   cups 1% low-fat milk
½   cup fat-free egg substitute
1   tablespoon dark rum
24   reduced-fat vanilla wafers, divided
2   cups sliced ripe banana (about 2 medium), divided
1   cup frozen fat-free whipped topping, thawed
2   tablespoons flaked coconut, toasted

1. Combine first 3 ingredients in a medium saucepan; gradually add milk and egg substitute, stirring until smooth. Bring mixture to a boil over medium heat, stirring constantly; boil 1 minute, stirring constantly. Remove from heat; stir in rum. Set pudding aside to cool.

2. Spread ½ cup pudding in bottom of a 1½-quart baking dish; arrange 12 vanilla wafers over pudding. Top with 1 cup banana slices.

3. Spread half of remaining pudding over banana; top with remaining 12 wafers, banana, and pudding. Cover and chill.

4. Spread whipped topping evenly over pudding. Sprinkle with coconut. Yield: 8 (½-cup) servings.

 COOKING SECRET: Substitute ¼ teaspoon rum extract for the dark rum, if desired.

Chocolate Chip Cookies
(recipe, page 59)

Oatmeal-Raisin Cookies
(recipe, page 60)

Blackberry Cobbler
(recipe, page 51)

Vanilla Ice Cream
(recipe, page 47)

Strawberry Shortcake
(recipe, page 55)

Chocolate Cream Pie
(recipe, page 48)

Mocha Fudge Pudding (photo, page 3)

½   cup sugar
3   tablespoons cornstarch
3   tablespoons unsweetened cocoa
⅛   teaspoon salt
2¼ cups fat-free milk
½   cup fat-free egg substitute
2   tablespoons Kahlúa
2   teaspoons vanilla extract
1   tablespoon reduced-calorie stick margarine

1. Combine first 4 ingredients in a medium saucepan; gradually add milk and egg substitute, stirring until smooth.

2. Bring mixture to a boil over medium heat, stirring constantly; boil 1 minute, stirring constantly. Add Kahlúa and vanilla; cook over low heat 1 minute.

3. Remove from heat; stir in margarine. Spoon pudding into 6 individual dessert dishes. Cover and chill thoroughly. Yield: 6 (½-cup) servings.

COOKING SECRET: Strong brewed coffee can be substituted in equal measure for the Kahlúa in this rich, creamy pudding.

POINTS:
3

EXCHANGES:
2 Starch

PER SERVING:
Calories 163
Carbohydrate 27.9g
Fat 1.8g (saturated 0.3g)
Fiber 0.0g
Protein 5.8g
Cholesterol 2mg
Sodium 145mg
Calcium 120mg
Iron 0.9mg

Stirred Vanilla Custard

POINTS:

3

EXCHANGES:

1½ Starch

½ Fat

PER SERVING:

Calories 141

Carbohydrate 24.2g

Fat 2.0g (saturated 0.7g)

Fiber 0.1g

Protein 6.4g

Cholesterol 76mg

Sodium 132mg

Calcium 155mg

Iron 0.4mg

3 cups fat-free milk
2 large eggs
½ cup sugar
1½ tablespoons all-purpose flour
⅛ teaspoon salt
1 teaspoon vanilla extract
Ground nutmeg (optional)

1. Heat milk in a heavy saucepan over low heat until very hot, stirring occasionally (do not boil).

2. Meanwhile, beat eggs at medium speed of an electric mixer until foamy. Add sugar, flour, and salt, beating until thick. Gradually stir about 1 cup hot milk into egg mixture; add to remaining hot mixture, stirring constantly.

3. Cook, stirring constantly, over medium heat 7 minutes or until thickened. Remove from heat, and stir in vanilla. Spoon ½ cup custard into individual dessert bowls. Sprinkle ground nutmeg lightly over each serving, if desired. Serve custard warm or chilled. Yield: 6 (½-cup) servings.

COOKING SECRET: This creamy custard has a consistency similar to eggnog. Spoon it over fresh melon or mixed berries for a special dessert.

Vanilla Ice Cream (photo, page 42)

2 tablespoons vanilla extract
1 tablespoon crème de cacao (optional)
1½ teaspoons unflavored gelatin
1 (14-ounce) can fat-free sweetened condensed milk
2 egg yolks, lightly beaten
⅛ teaspoon salt
3 cups 1% low-fat milk, divided

1. Combine vanilla and crème de cacao, if desired, in a small bowl; sprinkle gelatin over vanilla mixture, and set aside to soften.

2. Combine condensed milk, egg yolks, and salt in a small bowl; stir well with a whisk. Set aside. Heat 1½ cups milk in a heavy saucepan over medium heat until very hot (do not boil). Slowly add condensed milk mixture to milk in saucepan, stirring constantly. Cook, stirring constantly, 3 to 5 minutes or until mixture coats back of spoon (do not boil).

3. Add gelatin mixture to milk mixture; stir with a whisk until gelatin dissolves. Stir in remaining 1½ cups milk. Pour into a medium bowl; cover and chill at least 2 hours.

4. Pour mixture into freezer can of an electric ice cream freezer. Freeze according to manufacturer's instructions.

5. Pack freezer with additional ice and rock salt, and let stand 1 hour before serving. Yield: 8 (½-cup) servings.

🌿 COOKING SECRET: Crème de cacao is a dark, chocolate-flavored liqueur with a hint of vanilla. It gives this ice cream a wonderful flavor, but it may be omitted, if desired.

POINTS:
4

EXCHANGES:
1½ Starch
1 Skim Milk

PER SERVING:
Calories 203
Carbohydrate 35.0g
Fat 2.3g (saturated 1.0g)
Fiber 0.0g
Protein 7.9g
Cholesterol 59mg
Sodium 135mg
Calcium 244mg
Iron 0.2mg

Chocolate Cream Pie (photo, page 44)

POINTS:

6

EXCHANGES:

3 Starch

1½ Fat

PER SERVING:

Calories 282

Carbohydrate 44.3g

Fat 8.4g (saturated 3.3g)

Fiber 0.0g

Protein 4.3g

Cholesterol 6.3mg

Sodium 249mg

Calcium 80mg

Iron 0.6mg

½ (15-ounce) package refrigerated piecrusts
½ cup sugar
¼ cup cornstarch
¼ cup unsweetened cocoa
¼ teaspoon salt
2 cups fat-free milk
¼ cup fat-free egg substitute
1 tablespoon reduced-calorie stick margarine
1 teaspoon vanilla extract
1 (8-ounce) container frozen fat-free whipped topping, thawed

Grated chocolate (optional)

1. Fit piecrust into a 9-inch pie plate, and bake according to package directions. Set aside.

2. While crust bakes, combine sugar and next 3 ingredients in a heavy saucepan; gradually stir in milk. Bring mixture to a boil over medium heat, stirring constantly. Boil 1 minute, stirring constantly.

3. Gradually stir about one-fourth of hot mixture into egg substitute; add to remaining hot mixture, stirring constantly. Cook, stirring constantly, 1 minute. Remove from heat; stir in margarine and vanilla. Pour mixture into baked pastry shell; cover surface with plastic wrap, and chill at least 3 hours.

4. Spoon whipped topping evenly over filling, and garnish with grated chocolate, if desired. Yield: 8 servings.

COOKING SECRET: Pressing plastic wrap directly onto the surface of the filling prevents a thick skin from forming as the filling cools.

Coconut Cream Pie

1½ cups crushed chocolate graham crackers (about 11
    rectangles)
1   tablespoon sugar
¼   cup reduced-calorie stick margarine, melted
½   cup sugar
⅓   cup cornstarch
3   cups fat-free milk
½   cup fat-free egg substitute
⅔   cup sweetened flaked coconut
1½ teaspoons vanilla extract
½   teaspoon coconut extract
½   (8-ounce) container frozen fat-free whipped topping,
    thawed
1   tablespoon semisweet chocolate mini-morsels

1. Combine graham cracker crumbs and 1 tablespoon sugar. Stir in melted margarine. Press on bottom and up sides of a 9-inch pie plate. Bake at 350° for 10 minutes.

2. Combine ½ cup sugar and cornstarch in a medium saucepan; stir well. Gradually stir in milk. Bring mixture to a boil over medium heat, stirring constantly. Boil 1 minute, stirring constantly. Stir about one-fourth of hot mixture into egg substitute; add to remaining hot mixture, stirring constantly. Cook until mixture is thoroughly heated (do not boil). Remove from heat. Stir in coconut and extracts. Pour mixture into prepared crust; cover surface with plastic wrap, and chill at least 3 hours.

3. Spoon whipped topping over filling. Sprinkle with chocolate mini-morsels. Yield: 8 servings.

POINTS:
7

EXCHANGES:
3½ Starch
1½ Fat

PER SERVING:
Calories 308
Carbohydrate 50.3g
Fat 8.8g (saturated 3.5g)
Fiber 1.0g
Protein 6.2g
Cholesterol 2mg
Sodium 279mg
Calcium 121mg
Iron 1.3mg

Pumpkin Pie

POINTS:

5

EXCHANGES:

2½ Starch

1½ Fat

PER SERVING:

Calories 239

Carbohydrate 35.5g

Fat 8.6g (saturated 3.5g)

Fiber 2.3g

Protein 4.9g

Cholesterol 61mg

Sodium 147mg

Calcium 91mg

Iron 1.3mg

½ (15-ounce) package refrigerated piecrusts
1 (15-ounce) can unsweetened pumpkin
½ cup sugar
2 tablespoons all-purpose flour
1½ teaspoons ground cinnamon
½ teaspoon ground ginger
⅛ teaspoon ground allspice
¾ cup fat-free evaporated milk
2 eggs, lightly beaten
½ cup frozen fat-free whipped topping, thawed

1. Fit piecrust into a 9-inch pie plate and bake according to package directions. Set aside.

2. While crust bakes, combine pumpkin and next 5 ingredients in a large bowl; stir in milk. Add beaten eggs; stir well. Pour into baked pastry shell. Bake at 350° for 45 minutes or until a knife inserted in center comes out clean. Cool on a wire rack. Cover and store in refrigerator. Serve each slice with 1 tablespoon whipped topping. Yield: 8 servings.

 COOKING SECRET: The blend of spices gives this pumpkin pie a wonderful flavor.

Blackberry Cobbler (photo, page 42)

6 cups fresh blackberries
½ cup sugar
2 tablespoons orange juice
1½ tablespoons tapioca
¼ teaspoon ground allspice
1 cup all-purpose flour
1¼ teaspoons baking powder
¼ teaspoon baking soda
¼ teaspoon salt
⅓ cup sugar
⅓ cup vanilla low-fat yogurt
⅓ cup fat-free milk
3 tablespoons reduced-calorie stick margarine, softened
1 tablespoon sugar

1. Combine first 5 ingredients; toss gently to coat. Spoon mixture into an 11- x 7-inch baking dish.

2. Combine flour and next 4 ingredients in a bowl; stir well. Add yogurt, milk, and margarine; beat at medium speed of an electric mixer until smooth. Pour over blackberry mixture.

3. Bake at 350° for 20 minutes. Sprinkle 1 tablespoon sugar evenly over cobbler. Bake an additional 25 minutes or until crust is golden. Serve warm. Yield: 10 (½-cup) servings.

 TIP: A scoop of Vanilla Ice Cream (page 47) complements this old-fashioned dessert favorite.

POINTS:

3

EXCHANGES:

2 Starch
1 Fruit
½ Fat

PER SERVING:

Calories 202
Carbohydrate 43.7g
Fat 2.8g (saturated 0.4g)
Fiber 5.8g
Protein 2.7g
Cholesterol 0.7mg
Sodium 194mg
Calcium 92mg
Iron 1.3mg

Double Cherry Crisp

POINTS:

3

EXCHANGES:

2 Fruit

PER SERVING:

Calories 152

Carbohydrate 33.4g

Fat 1.0g (saturated 0.1g)

Fiber 2.7g

Protein 1.3g

Cholesterol 0mg

Sodium 68mg

Calcium 22mg

Iron 0.4mg

2   (21-ounce) cans light cherry pie filling
¾   cup dried cherries, coarsely chopped
1   teaspoon grated lemon rind
2   cups coarsely crumbled angel food cake
2   tablespoons brown sugar
2   tablespoons chopped almonds

1. Combine cherry pie filling, dried cherries, and lemon rind in an 8-inch square baking dish.

2. Combine crumbled cake, brown sugar, and almonds in a small bowl; sprinkle evenly over cherry mixture. Bake at 375° for 25 to 30 minutes or until topping is golden and filling is bubbly. Serve warm. Yield: 8 (½-cup) servings.

COOKING SECRET: Make coarsely crumbled angel food cake by tearing the cake into small pieces or putting cubed cake into a food processor and pulsing several times.

PREP: 30 minutes COOK: 35 minutes

Carrot Cake

2 cups all-purpose flour
⅓ cup unprocessed wheat bran
1 teaspoon baking powder
1 teaspoon baking soda
2 teaspoons ground cinnamon
1½ cups sugar
3 cups shredded carrot
1 (8-ounce) carton lemon nonfat yogurt
1 cup fat-free egg substitute
⅓ cup vegetable oil
Cooking spray
Lemon-Cream Cheese Frosting

1. Combine flour and next 5 ingredients in a large bowl; stir in carrot.

2. Combine yogurt, egg substitute, and oil in a small bowl; add to dry ingredients, stirring just until moistened.

3. Pour batter into a 13- x 9-inch baking pan coated with cooking spray. Bake at 350° for 35 to 40 minutes or until a wooden pick inserted in center comes out clean. Cool completely in pan on a wire rack. Spread Lemon-Cream Cheese Frosting over cooled cake. Yield: 24 servings.

Lemon-Cream Cheese Frosting
½ (8-ounce) package ⅓-less-fat cream cheese, softened
2 teaspoons vanilla extract
½ teaspoon grated lemon rind
3¼ cups sifted powdered sugar
2 to 3 teaspoons fat-free milk

1. Beat cream cheese, vanilla, and lemon rind at medium speed of an electric mixer until creamy; add powdered sugar, beating until smooth. Beat in milk, 1 teaspoon at a time, to reach desired consistency. Yield: 1½ cups.

POINTS:
4

EXCHANGES:
2½ Starch
1 Fat

PER SERVING:
Calories 208
Carbohydrate 39.9g
Fat 4.3g (saturated 1.3g)
Fiber 1.1g
Protein 3.2g
Cholesterol 4mg
Sodium 118mg
Calcium 42mg
Iron 0.9mg

Orange Pound Cake

POINTS:
4

EXCHANGES:
1½ Starch
1½ Fat

PER SERVING:
Calories 168
Carbohydrate 23.6g
Fat 7.5g (saturated 1.4g)
Fiber 0.2g
Protein 1.8g
Cholesterol 0mg
Sodium 109mg
Calcium 39mg
Iron 1.1mg

Cooking spray
1¾ cups sifted cake flour
2 teaspoons baking powder
¼ teaspoon salt
¾ cup sugar
½ cup vegetable oil
1 teaspoon grated orange rind
½ cup fresh orange juice
½ cup fat-free egg substitute
½ cup sifted powdered sugar
2 teaspoons fresh orange juice

1. Coat bottom of an 8½- x 4½-inch loafpan with cooking spray; dust with flour, and set aside.

2. Combine sifted cake flour and next 3 ingredients in a large bowl; make a well in center of mixture. Add oil and next 3 ingredients; beat at medium speed of an electric mixer until batter is smooth.

3. Pour batter into prepared pan. Bake at 350° for 40 minutes or until a wooden pick inserted in center comes out clean. Cool cake in pan 10 minutes; remove from pan. Cool cake completely on a wire rack.

4. Combine powdered sugar and 2 teaspoons orange juice; drizzle over cooled cake. Yield: 16 servings (1 slice per serving).

 COOKING SECRET: Substitute all-purpose flour for cake flour by using 2 tablespoons less all-purpose flour per cup.

Strawberry Shortcake (photo, page 43)

3 cups sliced fresh strawberries

4 tablespoons sugar, divided

3 tablespoons red currant jelly

1½ tablespoons water

2 cups plus 1 tablespoon low-fat biscuit and baking mix, divided

⅔ cup 1% low-fat milk

½ teaspoon vanilla extract

Cooking spray

1 tablespoon stick margarine, melted

1 tablespoon plus 1 teaspoon cinnamon-sugar

Frozen fat-free whipped topping, thawed (optional)

1. Combine strawberries and 1 tablespoon sugar; let stand 30 minutes. Combine jelly and water in a small saucepan; place over low heat. Cook, stirring until jelly melts. Remove from heat, and stir into strawberry mixture. Cover and chill.

2. Combine remaining 3 tablespoons sugar, 2 cups biscuit and baking mix, milk, and vanilla in a medium bowl; stir just until blended. Sprinkle remaining 1 tablespoon biscuit mix evenly over work surface. Turn dough out onto work surface; roll to ¾-inch thickness. Cut with a 2½-inch biscuit cutter, dipping cutter into additional biscuit mix to prevent sticking, if necessary.

3. Place shortcakes on a baking sheet coated with cooking spray. Brush tops with melted margarine; sprinkle with cinnamon-sugar. Bake at 425° for 12 to 15 minutes or until golden.

4. Split shortcakes in half. Place bottom halves on individual serving plates; top each with ½ cup strawberry mixture. Arrange remaining cake halves over strawberries. Garnish with 1 table-spoon whipped topping, if desired. Yield: 6 servings.

POINTS:

5

EXCHANGES:

2½ Starch

½ Fruit

1 Fat

PER SERVING:

Calories 249

Carbohydrate 46.3g

Fat 5.2g (saturated 1.1g)

Fiber 2.0g

Protein 4.5g

Cholesterol 1mg

Sodium 515mg

Calcium 69mg

Iron 1.2mg

Caramel-Apple Bread Pudding

POINTS:

5

EXCHANGES:

3 Starch

PER SERVING:

Calories 239
Carbohydrate 48.0g
Fat 1.7g (saturated 0.5g)
Fiber 1.6g
Protein 6.9g
Cholesterol 2mg
Sodium 350mg
Calcium 120mg
Iron 1.5mg

1½ cups 1% low-fat milk
1   cup unsweetened applesauce
½   cup firmly packed brown sugar
½   cup fat-free evaporated milk
½   cup fat-free egg substitute
2   teaspoons apple pie spice
1   teaspoon vanilla extract
8   cups (1-inch) French bread cubes
Cooking spray
¾   cup fat-free caramel ice cream topping

1. Combine first 7 ingredients in a large bowl; stir well. Add bread cubes, tossing to coat. Let stand 15 minutes.

2. Spoon bread mixture into an 11- x 7-inch baking dish coated with cooking spray. Bake at 325° for 55 minutes or until pudding is set and golden. Let stand 15 minutes. Spoon ½ cup pudding into individual serving dishes, and drizzle each with 1 tablespoon warm caramel topping. Yield: 12 servings.

TIME-SAVING TIP: Assemble the bread pudding a day ahead and refrigerate. Bake it the next evening while you cook dinner.

Gingerbread with Citrus Sauce

1¼ cups all-purpose flour
¼ cup unprocessed wheat bran
½ teaspoon baking powder
½ teaspoon baking soda
1 teaspoon ground ginger
1 teaspoon ground cinnamon
¼ cup firmly packed brown sugar
1 teaspoon grated lemon rind
½ cup water
½ cup molasses
¼ cup margarine, melted
¼ cup fat-free egg substitute
Cooking spray
Citrus Sauce

POINTS:
3

EXCHANGES:
2 Starch
1 Fat

PER SERVING:
Calories 159
Carbohydrate 29.5g
Fat 4.1g (saturated 0.8g)
Fiber 1.0g
Protein 2.2g
Cholesterol 0mg
Sodium 132mg
Calcium 52mg
Iron 1.7mg

1. Combine first 8 ingredients in a large mixing bowl. Combine water and next 3 ingredients in a small bowl. Add to dry ingredients; stir just until moistened.

2. Pour batter into an 8-inch square pan coated with cooking spray. Bake at 350° for 30 to 40 minutes or until a wooden pick inserted in center comes out clean. Cool slightly on a wire rack.

3. To serve, cut gingerbread into squares. Spoon Citrus Sauce over gingerbread. Yield: 12 servings (1 square cake and 2 teaspoons sauce per serving).

Citrus Sauce
3 tablespoons sugar
2 teaspoons cornstarch
½ cup orange juice
1 tablespoon lemon juice

1. Combine sugar and cornstarch in a small saucepan. Stir in orange juice and lemon juice. Cook over medium heat, stirring constantly, until mixture thickens. Boil 1 minute. Yield: ½ cup.

Buttermilk Brownies with Chocolate-Mint Glaze

POINTS:
3

EXCHANGES:
1½ Starch
1 Fat

PER SERVING:
Calories 134
Carbohydrate 21.9g
Fat 4.3g (saturated 1.0g)
Fiber 0.2g
Protein 2.3g
Cholesterol 0mg
Sodium 98mg
Calcium 24mg
Iron 0.9mg

¾   cup all-purpose flour
¼   teaspoon baking powder
¼   teaspoon baking soda
¼   cup stick margarine
⅔   cup sugar
¼   cup unsweetened cocoa
¼   cup fat-free egg substitute
½   teaspoon vanilla extract
⅓   cup low-fat buttermilk
Cooking spray
Chocolate-Mint Glaze

1. Combine first 3 ingredients in a small bowl; set aside.

2. Melt margarine in a medium saucepan over medium-low heat. Stir in sugar and cocoa. Remove from heat, and cool 5 minutes. Stir in egg substitute and vanilla. Add flour mixture alternately with buttermilk, stirring just until combined, beginning and ending with flour mixture. Spoon into a 9-inch square pan coated with cooking spray. Bake at 350° for 15 minutes or until a wooden pick inserted in center comes out clean. Cool completely. Drizzle Chocolate-Mint Glaze over cooled brownies. Cut into bars. Yield: 12 servings.

Chocolate-Mint Glaze

⅓   cup sifted powdered sugar
1   tablespoon unsweetened cocoa
⅛   teaspoon peppermint extract
2   to 3 teaspoons fat-free milk

1. Combine powdered sugar and cocoa. Stir in peppermint extract. Add milk, 1 teaspoon at a time, stirring until mixture is glazing consistency. Yield: ⅓ cup.

PREP: 23 minutes COOK: 10 minutes

Chocolate Chip Cookies (photo, page 41)

2⅓ cups all-purpose flour
½ teaspoon baking soda
1 cup firmly packed brown sugar
¾ cup stick margarine, softened
½ cup sugar
½ cup fat-free egg substitute
2 teaspoons vanilla extract
1¼ cups semisweet chocolate mini-morsels

1. Combine flour and soda in a large bowl; set aside.

2. Beat brown sugar, margarine, and sugar at medium speed of an electric mixer until blended. Add egg substitute and vanilla, beating well. Gradually add dry ingredients, beating well. Stir in chocolate morsels.

3. Drop dough by rounded tablespoonfuls onto ungreased baking sheets. Bake at 350° for 10 minutes or until golden. Remove cookies from baking sheets, and let cool completely on wire racks. Yield: 4 dozen (1 cookie per serving).

COOKING SECRET: Using semisweet chocolate mini-morsels guarantees you'll find a chocolate chip in every bite of these cookies.

POINTS:
2

EXCHANGES:
1 Starch
1 Fat

PER SERVING:
Calories 104
Carbohydrate 15.0g
Fat 4.6g (saturated 1.6g)
Fiber 0.5g
Protein 0.9g
Cholesterol 0mg
Sodium 52mg
Calcium 7mg
Iron 0.4mg

Oatmeal-Raisin Cookies (photo, page 41)

POINTS:
2

EXCHANGES:
1 Starch
½ Fat

PER SERVING:
Calories 78
Carbohydrate 14.1g
Fat 2.1g (saturated 0.4g)
Fiber 0.6g
Protein 1.2g
Cholesterol 0mg
Sodium 43mg
Calcium 7mg
Iron 0.5mg

¾ cup sugar
¼ cup firmly packed brown sugar
⅓ cup stick margarine, softened
¼ cup apple butter
¼ cup fat-free egg substitute
½ teaspoon vanilla extract
½ teaspoon ground cinnamon
½ teaspoon baking soda
1½ cups quick-cooking oats
1 cup all-purpose flour
½ cup raisins
Cooking spray

1. Beat first 3 ingredients in a large bowl at medium speed of an electric mixer until blended. Add apple butter and next 4 ingredients; beating well. Stir in oats, flour, and raisins.

2. Drop dough by rounded tablespoonfuls onto baking sheets coated with cooking spray. Bake at 375° for 9 minutes or until lightly browned. Cool 1 minute on baking sheets. Remove cookies from baking sheets, and let cool completely on wire racks. Yield: 34 cookies (1 cookie per serving).

COOKING SECRET: If you bake cookies often, invest in sturdy, shiny aluminum baking sheets, large wire cooling racks, and a good metal spatula.

fish
&
shellfish

Baked Catfish

POINTS:
4

EXCHANGES:
½ Starch
3 Very Lean Meat

PER SERVING:
Calories 172
Carbohydrate 9.6g
Fat 5.6g (saturated 1.2g)
Fiber 1.1g
Protein 21.7g
Cholesterol 66mg
Sodium 368mg
Calcium 71mg
Iron 1.9mg

¼ cup cornmeal
1 teaspoon dried basil
1 teaspoon garlic powder
½ teaspoon dried thyme
½ teaspoon salt
¼ teaspoon freshly ground pepper
4 (4-ounce) farm-raised catfish fillets
Cooking spray
1 lemon, quartered (optional)

1. Combine first 6 ingredients in a heavy-duty, zip-top plastic bag. Add fish; seal bag, and turn gently to coat. Place fish on a baking sheet coated with cooking spray. Coat fish lightly with cooking spray.

2. Bake on bottom rack of oven at 400° for 10 minutes on each side; reduce heat to 350° and bake 5 additional minutes or until crust is golden and fish flakes easily when tested with a fork. Serve with lemon wedges, if desired. Yield: 4 servings.

 FOR A QUICK MEAL: Serve this entrée with Crunchy Coleslaw (page 135).

Grilled Salmon with Teriyaki Sauce

¼ cup dry sherry
¼ cup low-sodium soy sauce
1 tablespoon brown sugar
1 tablespoon rice wine vinegar
1 teaspoon garlic powder
½ teaspoon freshly ground pepper
⅛ teaspoon ground ginger
1 (16-ounce) skinless salmon fillet (1 inch thick)
Cooking spray

POINTS:
4

EXCHANGES:
3½ Lean Meat

PER SERVING:
Calories 190
Carbohydrate 4.8g
Fat 6.9g (saturated 1.3g)
Fiber 0.1g
Protein 25.5g
Cholesterol 44mg
Sodium 548mg
Calcium 21mg
Iron 1.3mg

1. Combine first 7 ingredients in a shallow dish; stir well. Add fish; cover, and marinate in refrigerator 30 minutes.

2. Coat grill rack with cooking spray; place on grill over medium-hot coals (350° to 400°). Remove fish from marinade; reserve marinade. Place fish on grill rack or in a grill basket coated with cooking spray; grill, uncovered, 5 to 7 minutes on each side or until fish flakes easily when tested with a fork. Transfer fish to a serving platter, and keep warm.

3. Place reserved marinade in a small saucepan; bring to a boil. Boil 5 minutes or until marinade becomes thick and syrupy. Spoon over fish; serve immediately. Yield: 4 servings.

FOR A QUICK MEAL: This easy salmon entrée received our highest rating. Serve it on a bed of couscous alongside mixed salad greens, and for dessert, fresh fruit.

Trout with Almonds

POINTS:
7

EXCHANGES:
½ Starch
3½ Lean Meat
1 Fat

PER SERVING:
Calories 281
Carbohydrate 8.5g
Fat 15.6g (saturated 2.5g)
Fiber 1.3g
Protein 26.1g
Cholesterol 66mg
Sodium 275mg
Calcium 75mg
Iron 2.5mg

¼ cup all-purpose flour
¼ teaspoon salt
¼ teaspoon pepper
4 (4-ounce) trout fillets
3 tablespoons yogurt-based spread (such as Brummel & Brown), divided
2 tablespoons fresh lemon juice
2 tablespoons chopped fresh parsley
¼ cup slivered almonds, toasted

1. Combine first 3 ingredients in a large heavy-duty, zip-top plastic bag. Add fish; seal bag, and turn gently to coat.

2. Heat 1 tablespoon spread in a large nonstick skillet over medium-high heat. Add fish to skillet; cook, turning once, 5 to 6 minutes, or until fish flakes easily when tested with a fork. Set fish aside, and keep warm.

3. Add remaining 2 tablespoons spread, lemon juice, and parsley to skillet. Bring to a simmer. Spoon sauce over fish; sprinkle with almonds. Yield: 4 servings (1 fish fillet, 1 tablespoon sauce, and 1 tablespoon almonds per serving).

TIP: This recipe is higher in fat than most fish entrées, but the fats are mostly monounsaturated and polyunsaturated, the heart-healthy types of fat. Compare the 15.6 grams of fat in one serving of this dish to a traditional trout amandine, which has about 54 grams of fat per serving.

Tuna Casserole

5 ounces uncooked medium egg noodles
1 (10¾-ounce) can reduced-fat, reduced-sodium cream of mushroom soup, undiluted (such as Campbell's Healthy Request)
1 (8.5-ounce) can English peas, drained
1 (6-ounce) can solid white tuna in spring water, drained and flaked
1 (5-ounce) can fat-free evaporated milk
¾ cup (3 ounces) shredded reduced-fat Cheddar cheese
⅓ cup finely chopped onion
½ teaspoon pepper
Cooking spray
⅔ cup crushed reduced-fat cheese crackers (about 47 crackers)

1. Cook noodles according to package directions, omitting salt and fat; drain. Combine noodles, soup, and next 6 ingredients; pour into an 8-inch square baking dish coated with cooking spray.

2. Cover and bake at 350° for 30 minutes. Sprinkle with crushed crackers; bake, uncovered, 10 more minutes or until thoroughly heated. Serve immediately. Yield: 4 (1-cup) servings.

FOR A QUICK MEAL: This dish is a complete meal in itself, but if you like, serve it with a tossed green salad and for dessert, Caramel-Apple Bread Pudding (page 56).

POINTS:
8

EXCHANGES:
3 Starch
3 Lean Meat

PER SERVING:
Calories 399
Carbohydrate 46.7g
Fat 10.2g (saturated 4.6g)
Fiber 2.2g
Protein 29.9g
Cholesterol 74mg
Sodium 916mg
Calcium 301mg
Iron 2.8mg

Crab Cakes (photo, page 78)

POINTS:

6

EXCHANGES:

1 Starch
3½ Lean Meat

PER SERVING:

Calories 270
Carbohydrate 17.6g
Fat 9.0g (saturated 1.9g)
Fiber 0.9g
Protein 28.0g
Cholesterol 175mg
Sodium 735mg
Calcium 209mg
Iron 3.2mg

1	pound fresh lump crabmeat, drained
¾	cup fine, dry breadcrumbs
¼	cup reduced-fat mayonnaise
1	tablespoon grated Parmesan cheese
1¼	teaspoons Italian seasoning
1½	teaspoons Worcestershire sauce
⅛	teaspoon salt
⅛	teaspoon freshly ground pepper
1	large egg, lightly beaten
2	to 3 green onions, thinly sliced (about ⅓ cup)
1	medium jalapeño pepper, seeded and diced

Cooking spray
Lemon wedges (optional)
Cocktail sauce (optional)

1. Combine first 11 ingredients in a large bowl. Form into 8 patties, and place on a baking sheet coated with cooking spray.

2. Bake at 400° for 5 minutes on each side or until golden. Serve with lemon wedges and cocktail sauce, if desired. Yield: 4 servings (2 crab cakes per serving).

 FOR A QUICK MEAL: These crab cakes are hearty, so serve them with a simple tossed salad.

Sweet-and-Sour Shrimp with Rice

1   teaspoon vegetable oil

1   pound peeled, deveined medium-size fresh shrimp

Cooking spray

2   medium-size green peppers, seeded and cut into 1-inch
        pieces (about 3 cups)

1   medium onion, cut into wedges and separated (about
        2 cups)

1   (13-ounce) can pineapple chunks in juice, drained

¾   cup sweet-and-sour sauce

3   cups hot cooked rice, cooked without salt or fat

1. Add oil to a large nonstick skillet or wok, and place over high
heat until hot. Add shrimp to skillet, and stir-fry 3 minutes or
until shrimp turn pink. Remove shrimp from skillet, and
keep warm.

2. Coat skillet with cooking spray. Add green pepper and onion;
stir-fry 4 minutes. Add reserved shrimp and pineapple chunks.
Stir in sweet-and-sour sauce. Reduce heat to low, and cook, stirring constantly, 2 minutes. Serve over rice. Yield: 4 servings (1¼
cups shrimp mixture and ¾ cup rice per serving).

TIME-SAVING TIP: To cut down on preparation, have
someone in your supermarket's seafood department peel
and devein the shrimp while you shop.

POINTS:

6

EXCHANGES:

2 Starch

1 Vegetable

1 Fruit

2 Very Lean Meat

PER SERVING:

Calories 298

Carbohydrate 49.1g

Fat 3.3g (saturated 0.6g)

Fiber 2.9g

Protein 19.9g

Cholesterol 129mg

Sodium 182mg

Calcium 74mg

Iron 3.9mg

Seafood Paella (photo, page 77)

POINTS:
6

EXCHANGES:
2½ Starch
1 Vegetable
1 Lean Meat

PER SERVING:
Calories 279
Carbohydrate 42.4g
Fat 4.6g (saturated 0.7g)
Fiber 1.7g
Protein 16.3g
Cholesterol 48mg
Sodium 673mg
Calcium 31mg
Iron 2.9mg

6 cups ⅓-less-salt chicken broth (such as Swanson's Natural Goodness)
½ teaspoon saffron threads, crumbled, or ⅛ teaspoon ground saffron
⅛ teaspoon freshly ground black pepper
¼ teaspoon paprika
2 tablespoons olive oil
1¼ cups diced green pepper (about 1 large)
1 cup sliced onion (about 1 small)
3 cloves garlic, minced
1½ cups Arborio or short-grain rice
½ pound peeled, deveined medium-size fresh shrimp
½ pound bay scallops
2 cups diced plum tomatoes (about 4)
1 (11-ounce) can Mexican-style corn

1. Combine first 4 ingredients in a medium saucepan. Bring to a boil, reduce heat, and simmer 10 minutes.

2. Meanwhile, heat olive oil in a large nonstick skillet over medium-high heat. Add green pepper, onion, and garlic; cook 3 to 5 minutes, stirring constantly, until lightly browned. Add rice and cook 1 minute, stirring constantly. Stir in broth mixture and simmer, uncovered, 20 minutes, stirring occasionally. Stir in shrimp and remaining ingredients. Simmer, uncovered, 10 minutes, or until liquid is absorbed. Remove from heat; cover, and let stand 5 minutes. Yield: 8 (1-cup) servings.

 TIP: If you are preparing this paella for a party, leave the tails on the shrimp for an attractive presentation.

meatless main dishes

Fettuccine Alfredo (photo, page 80)

POINTS:

7

EXCHANGES:

3½ Starch
1 High-Fat Meat

PER SERVING:

Calories 348
Carbohydrate 50.5g
Fat 7.5g (saturated 3.6g)
Fiber 1.1g
Protein 15.7g
Cholesterol 88mg
Sodium 604mg
Calcium 256mg
Iron 2.2mg

1 (12-ounce) package spinach and egg fettuccine noodles
1 teaspoon butter
4 to 5 cloves garlic, divided
½ cup dry white wine
2 cups fat-free half-and-half or fat-free evaporated milk, divided
2 tablespoons all-purpose flour
½ teaspoon salt
¼ teaspoon freshly ground pepper
1¼ cups freshly grated Parmesan cheese

1. Cook pasta according to package directions, omitting salt and fat; drain, and keep warm.

2. While pasta cooks, melt butter in a small saucepan over medium heat. Thinly slice 2 cloves garlic; add to butter. Cook 2 minutes, stirring constantly, until lightly browned. Increase heat to medium-high; add wine, and bring to a simmer. Cook 5 minutes or until mixture is reduced by half.

3. Combine 2 tablespoons half-and-half and flour, stirring until smooth. Add flour mixture to wine mixture; add remaining half-and-half, stirring well. Cook, stirring constantly, 5 minutes or until thickened. Stir in salt and pepper.

4. Pour half-and-half mixture over noodles; toss well. Mince remaining garlic; toss with noodle mixture, and stir in cheese. Garnish with additional pepper and cheese, if desired. Serve immediately. Yield: 6 (1-cup) servings.

FOR A QUICK MEAL: Pick up 1 (7.5-ounce) package of fat-free Caesar salad mix and strawberry sorbet to round out this creamy entrée.

Pasta Primavera

1 (9-ounce) package refrigerated fettuccine, uncooked
Cooking spray
1 cup broccoli flowerets
1 cup sliced carrot
1¼ cups thinly sliced zucchini (about 1 small)
1 cup sliced fresh mushrooms
2 cloves garlic, minced
1 (10-ounce) container refrigerated light alfredo sauce
2 tablespoons chopped fresh basil
½ teaspoon freshly ground pepper
¼ teaspoon salt
¼ cup freshly grated Parmesan cheese

POINTS:
7

EXCHANGES:
3 Starch
1 Vegetable
1 Medium-Fat Meat

PER SERVING:
Calories 334
Carbohydrate 47.1g
Fat 9.8g (saturated 6.0g)
Fiber 3.3g
Protein 16.2g
Cholesterol 90mg
Sodium 696mg
Calcium 231mg
Iron 2.2mg

1. Cook pasta according to package directions, omitting salt and fat; drain, and keep warm.

2. While pasta cooks, coat a large nonstick skillet with cooking spray; place over medium-high heat until hot. Add broccoli and carrot; cook, stirring constantly, 3 to 5 minutes or until tender. Add zucchini, mushrooms, and garlic; cook, stirring constantly, 5 additional minutes or until tender. Add alfredo sauce and next 3 ingredients to vegetable mixture; cook until thoroughly heated.

3. Pour sauce mixture over pasta; toss well. Sprinkle with cheese. Serve immediately. Yield: 4 (1½-cup) servings.

 FOR A QUICK MEAL: Soft breadsticks and fresh melon complement this one-dish meal.

Vegetable Lasagna

POINTS:
5

EXCHANGES:
1½ Starch
2 Vegetable
1 High-Fat Meat

PER SERVING:
Calories 247
Carbohydrate 34.6g
Fat 7.5g (saturated 3.8g)
Fiber 5.2g
Protein 14.9g
Cholesterol 23mg
Sodium 679mg
Calcium 319mg
Iron 2.9mg

Cooking spray
3   cups chopped zucchini
1   cup chopped onion
2   cups sliced fresh mushrooms
1   cup dry white wine, divided
¼   teaspoon salt
¼   teaspoon pepper
1   (16-ounce) container part-skim ricotta cheese
1   (10-ounce) package frozen chopped spinach, thawed,
      drained, and squeezed dry
¼   cup chopped fresh basil
4   cloves garlic, minced
1   (26-ounce) jar fresh tomato and basil pasta sauce (such as
      Five Brothers)
1   (14½-ounce) can diced tomatoes
10 uncooked lasagna noodles
1   cup (4 ounces) shredded part-skim mozzarella cheese

1. Coat a nonstick skillet with cooking spray; place over medium-high heat until hot. Add zucchini and onion; cook 5 to 7 minutes or until lightly browned, stirring occasionally. Add mushrooms, ½ cup wine, salt, and pepper. Reduce heat to medium, and cook 5 minutes or until liquid is absorbed and mushrooms are tender. Set aside.

2. Combine ricotta cheese and next 3 ingredients. Set aside.

3. Combine pasta sauce, tomatoes, and remaining ½ cup wine. Pour 1 cup sauce in bottom of a 13- x 9-inch baking dish coated with cooking spray. Place 3 lasagna noodles on top of sauce; top with cheese mixture and 3 lasagna noodles. Pour 1 cup sauce over noodles, and layer with cooked vegetables. Top with 4 remaining noodles and remaining sauce. Cover tightly, and bake at 350° for 1 hour and 15 minutes. Uncover and sprinkle with mozzarella cheese. Increase heat to 400° and bake, uncovered, 15 minutes or until cheese melts. Let stand 10 minutes before serving. Yield: 9 (1-cup) servings.

Macaroni and Cheese

6 ounces elbow macaroni, uncooked
Cooking spray
½ cup chopped onion
2 tablespoons reduced-calorie margarine
1 tablespoon all-purpose flour
1¼ cups fat-free milk
1½ cups (6 ounces) shredded reduced-fat sharp Cheddar cheese
¼ teaspoon salt
¼ teaspoon dry mustard
⅛ to ¼ teaspoon ground red pepper
Paprika (optional)

POINTS:
8

EXCHANGES:
2½ Starch
2 Medium-Fat Meat

PER SERVING:
Calories 342
Carbohydrate 36.7g
Fat 12.8g (saturated 5.4g)
Fiber 2.0g
Protein 20.2g
Cholesterol 30mg
Sodium 549mg
Calcium 478mg
Iron 1.7mg

1. Cook macaroni according to package directions, omitting salt and fat; drain.

2. While macaroni cooks, coat a small nonstick skillet with cooking spray; place over medium-high heat until hot. Add onion, and cook, stirring constantly, until tender. Set aside.

3. Melt margarine over low heat in a small saucepan; add flour, stirring until smooth. Gradually add milk, stirring constantly. Cook, stirring constantly, until thickened and bubbly. Remove from heat; add cheese and next 3 ingredients, stirring until cheese is melted.

4. Combine macaroni, onion, and cheese mixture; stir well. Spoon into a 2-quart baking dish coated with cooking spray. Sprinkle with paprika, if desired. Cover and bake at 350° for 15 minutes; uncover and bake 10 minutes or until bubbly. Yield: 6 (¾-cup) servings.

COOKING SECRET: If you shred the cheese yourself rather than using preshredded, you'll have creamier macaroni and cheese.

Baked Mostaccioli

POINTS:
8

EXCHANGES:
4 Starch
2 Vegetable
1 High-Fat Meat

PER SERVING:
Calories 431
Carbohydrate 69.6g
Fat 7.5g (saturated 2.7g)
Fiber 5.3g
Protein 22.7g
Cholesterol 13mg
Sodium 692mg
Calcium 257mg
Iron 4.5mg

1   (12-ounce) package mostaccioli or other tubular pasta
     Olive oil-flavored cooking spray
1   cup chopped onion
1½   cups chopped sweet red pepper
1½   cups chopped green pepper
2   cloves garlic, minced
½   cup dry white wine
1   (26-ounce) jar fire-roasted tomato and garlic pasta sauce
     (such as Classico)
1   cup (4 ounces) shredded part-skim mozzarella cheese
½   cup chopped vegetarian pepperoni (about 4 ounces)
¾   cup soft breadcrumbs
¼   cup freshly grated Parmesan cheese
1   clove garlic, minced

1. Cook pasta according to package directions, omitting salt and fat; rinse, and drain.

2. While pasta cooks, coat a large nonstick skillet with cooking spray; place over medium-high heat until hot. Add onion and next 3 ingredients. Cook 5 minutes or until vegetables are tender and lightly browned, stirring occasionally. Add wine and simmer, uncovered, 3 minutes. Add pasta sauce; cover, and simmer 10 minutes.

3. Combine pasta, sauce mixture, mozzarella cheese, and pepperoni. Spoon mixture into a 13- x 9-inch baking dish coated with cooking spray. Combine breadcrumbs, Parmesan cheese, and minced garlic. Sprinkle breadcrumb mixture over pasta. Bake, uncovered, at 375° for 20 minutes or until topping is lightly browned. Yield: 6 (1¼-cup) servings.

 TIP: Vegetarian pepperoni can be found in the produce section of most major grocery stores.

Spinach-Cheese-Stuffed Shells (photo, page 79)

½ (12-ounce) package jumbo shell pasta (about 20 shells)
¾ cup nonfat cottage cheese
¾ cup part-skim ricotta cheese
¾ cup shredded part-skim mozzarella cheese
1 (10-ounce) package frozen chopped spinach, thawed,
      drained, and squeezed dry
2 teaspoons dried basil
½ teaspoon ground nutmeg
⅛ teaspoon pepper
1 (26-ounce) jar fire-roasted tomato and garlic pasta sauce
      (such as Classico)
2 tablespoons grated Parmesan cheese

POINTS:
7

EXCHANGES:
2½ Starch
½ Vegetable
1 Lean Meat
1 Low-Fat Milk

PER SERVING:
Calories 389
Carbohydrate 51.6g
Fat 8.7g (saturated 4.2g)
Fiber 5.6g
Protein 24.2g
Cholesterol 25mg
Sodium 823mg
Calcium 420mg
Iron 3.6mg

1. Cook pasta according to package directions, omitting salt and fat. Rinse with cold water; drain.

2. While pasta cooks, combine cheeses, spinach, and next 3 ingredients in a large bowl; stir well. Fill pasta shells with mixture.

3. Spread ¾ cup pasta sauce in bottom of a 13- x 9-inch baking dish. Place stuffed shells in a single layer in dish; top with remaining sauce. Sprinkle with Parmesan cheese. Cover and bake at 350° for 30 minutes. Uncover and bake 5 additional minutes. Yield: 5 servings (4 shells per serving).

COOKING SECRET: To easily stuff the pasta shells, pour the spinach and cheese mixture into a heavy-duty, zip-top plastic bag; cut one corner off, and squeeze mixture into shells.

Bean-and-Corn Enchiladas

POINTS:
8

EXCHANGES:
4½ Starch
½ High-Fat Meat
1 Fat

PER SERVING:
Calories 413
Carbohydrate 67.3g
Fat 9.7g (saturated 3.5g)
Fiber 6.6g
Protein 18.5g
Cholesterol 19mg
Sodium 721mg
Calcium 416mg
Iron 2.8mg

1   (15-ounce) can pinto beans, rinsed and drained
1   (11-ounce) can sweet white and yellow corn, rinsed and drained
¼   cup grated onion
2   cloves garlic, minced
1¼ cups (5 ounces) shredded reduced-fat sharp Cheddar cheese, divided
2   (10-ounce) cans enchilada sauce, divided
15 soft corn tortillas
Cooking spray

1. Combine first 4 ingredients in a medium bowl. Stir in ½ cup cheese and ¼ cup enchilada sauce. Set aside.

2. Heat tortillas according to package directions. Spread about 2 tablespoons bean mixture down center of each tortilla, and roll up. Place enchiladas, seam sides down, in a 13- x 9-inch baking dish coated with cooking spray. Spread remaining enchilada sauce over enchiladas, and sprinkle with remaining ¾ cup cheese.

3. Cover and bake at 375° for 25 minutes or until bubbly. Yield: 5 servings (3 tortillas per serving).

FOR A QUICK MEAL: Baked tortilla chips with Guacamole (page 16) and Fresh Tomato Salsa (page 19) round out this meal.

Seafood Paella
(recipe, page 68)

Crab Cakes
(recipe, page 66)

Spinach-Cheese-
Stuffed Shells
(recipe, page 75)

Fettuccine Alfredo

Eggplant Parmigiana

½ cup fat-free egg substitute

¼ cup freshly grated Parmesan cheese, divided

¼ cup fat-free milk

1 cup Italian-seasoned breadcrumbs

1 (1-pound) eggplant, peeled and cut into ½-inch slices

2 tablespoons olive oil

Cooking spray

2 cups fire-roasted tomato and garlic pasta sauce (such as Classico)

1 cup (4 ounces) shredded part-skim mozzarella cheese

1. Combine egg substitute, 2 tablespoons Parmesan cheese, and milk in a shallow bowl, stirring well; set aside.

2. Place breadcrumbs in a shallow dish. Dip eggplant slices in egg mixture; dredge in breadcrumbs.

3. Heat oil in a large nonstick skillet over medium-high heat. Add eggplant slices, and cook 5 minutes on each side or until golden.

4. Arrange half of eggplant slices in an 11- x 7-inch baking dish coated with cooking spray. Spoon 1 cup pasta sauce over eggplant, and sprinkle with remaining 2 tablespoons Parmesan cheese. Repeat procedure with remaining eggplant and 1 cup sauce.

5. Bake, uncovered, at 350° for 25 minutes. Sprinkle with mozzarella cheese; bake an additional 5 to 10 minutes or until cheese melts. Yield: 6 (1-cup) servings.

 TIP: For an even heartier one-dish meal, serve this classic Italian entrée over spaghetti, cooked without salt or fat.

POINTS:

5

EXCHANGES:

1 Starch

2 Vegetable

1 Medium-Fat Meat

1 Fat

PER SERVING:

Calories 245

Carbohydrate 25.7g

Fat 10.0g (saturated 3.4g)

Fiber 3.0g

Protein 13.1g

Cholesterol 14mg

Sodium 977mg

Calcium 251mg

Iron 1.8mg

Sweet Pepper Pizza with Three Cheeses

POINTS:

4

EXCHANGES:

1½ Starch

1 Vegetable

1 Medium-Fat Meat

PER SERVING:

Calories 217

Carbohydrate 30.2g

Fat 6.3g (saturated 2.9g)

Fiber 2.3g

Protein 10.9g

Cholesterol 10mg

Sodium 413mg

Calcium 269mg

Iron 2.21mg

Olive oil-flavored cooking spray

½ (8-ounce) package sliced fresh mushrooms

1 (10-ounce) thin crust Italian bread shell (such as Boboli)

3 plum tomatoes, thinly sliced

1 small onion, thinly sliced and separated into rings

1 medium-size green or sweet red pepper, thinly sliced

2 tablespoons chopped fresh basil

3 tablespoons sliced ripe olives

1 cup (4 ounces) shredded part-skim mozzarella cheese

1 tablespoon grated Parmesan cheese

1 tablespoon grated Romano cheese

1. Coat a medium skillet with cooking spray. Place over medium-high heat until hot. Add mushrooms and cook, stirring constantly 5 minutes or until golden. Set aside.

2. Place bread shell on an ungreased baking sheet or pizza pan. Top bread shell with mushrooms, tomato, onion, pepper, basil, and olives; sprinkle with mozzerella, Parmesan, and Romano cheeses.

3. Bake at 475° for 6 to 9 minutes or until cheeses melt. Cut into 8 wedges. Yield: 8 servings.

FOR A QUICK MEAL: This hearty pizza is a veggie-lover's delight. Serve it with a tossed green salad and for dessert, fruit sorbet or Italian ice.

meats

Classic Hamburgers (photo, cover)

POINTS:
8

EXCHANGES:
2 Starch
1½ Vegetable
3½ Lean Meat

PER SERVING:
Calories 383
Carbohydrate 38.4g
Fat 10.5g (saturated 3.2g)
Fiber 4.2g
Protein 33.2g
Cholesterol 83mg
Sodium 531mg
Calcium 63mg
Iron 4.5mg

1	pound ground round
½	cup quick-cooking oats
¼	cup minced fresh parsley
1	tablespoon Dijon mustard
1	tablespoon Worcestershire sauce
½	teaspoon freshly ground pepper
2	cloves garlic, minced
1	small onion, minced (about ¾ cup)
1	egg white
Cooking spray	
4	leaves lettuce
4	whole wheat kaiser rolls, split
8	thin slices tomato
4	slices purple onion, separated into rings

1. Combine first 9 ingredients in a large bowl; stir well. Shape into 4 (¼-inch-thick) patties.

2. Coat grill rack with cooking spray; place on grill over medium-hot coals (350° to 400°). Place patties on rack; grill, covered, 5 minutes on each side or until done.

3. Place 1 lettuce leaf on bottom half of each roll; place patties on rolls. Top each patty with 2 slices of tomato and 1 slice of onion. Yield: 4 servings.

 FOR A QUICK MEAL: Cheese Fries (page 178) and Chocolate Cream Pie (page 48) round out the meal.

Salisbury Steak with Mushroom Gravy

1½ pounds ground round
1¾ cups soft breadcrumbs (about 4 slices bread)
½ cup chopped onion
¼ cup chopped green pepper
2 tablespoons steak sauce
1 egg white
½ teaspoon salt
½ teaspoon pepper
Mushroom Gravy

1. Combine first 8 ingredients in a large bowl; stir well. Shape into 6 patties. Place patties on a rack in broiler pan. Broil 5 inches from heat 6 minutes; turn patties. Broil 6 additional minutes or until done. Serve with Mushroom Gravy. Yield: 6 servings (1 patty and ¼ cup gravy per serving).

Mushroom Gravy

2 teaspoons reduced-calorie margarine
2 cups sliced fresh mushrooms
1 shallot, finely chopped
2 tablespoons all-purpose flour
¼ cup dry white wine
1 (14.25-ounce) can no-salt-added beef broth, undiluted
¼ teaspoon pepper
¼ teaspoon dried thyme

1. Melt margarine in a nonstick skillet over medium-high heat; add mushrooms and shallot, and cook 3 to 5 minutes or until golden, stirring constantly. Add flour, and cook 1 minute, stirring constantly. Add wine; reduce heat, and simmer, uncovered, 2 minutes. Add beef broth, pepper, and thyme; simmer, uncovered, 7 minutes or until mixture is reduced by one-fourth, stirring occasionally. Yield: 1½ cups.

POINTS:
5

EXCHANGES:
1 Starch
3½ Lean Meat

PER SERVING:
Calories 251
Carbohydrate 15.3g
Fat 7.3g (saturated 2.3g)
Fiber 1.2g
Protein 29.8g
Cholesterol 66mg
Sodium 499mg
Calcium 33mg
Iron 3.7mg

Favorite Meat Loaf

POINTS:
3

EXCHANGES:
½ Starch
2 Lean Meat

PER SERVING:
Calories 137
Carbohydrate 7.7g
Fat 4.1g (saturated 1.4g)
Fiber 1.2g
Protein 17.2g
Cholesterol 62mg
Sodium 213mg
Calcium 38mg
Iron 2.2mg

Cooking spray
½ cup chopped onion
¼ cup finely chopped celery
2   cloves garlic, minced
1½ pounds ground round
1   (14½-ounce) can diced tomatoes with Italian herbs, drained (such as Contadina)
3   (1-ounce) slices reduced-calorie whole wheat bread, torn into small pieces
1   tablespoon reduced-sodium Worcestershire sauce
¼ teaspoon pepper
1   large egg, lightly beaten
1   egg white, lightly beaten
2   tablespoons chili sauce
1   tablespoon water

1. Coat a nonstick skillet with cooking spray; place over medium-high heat until hot. Add onion, celery, and garlic; cook 3 minutes or until tender, stirring constantly.

2. Combine onion mixture, ground round, and next 6 ingredients in a bowl; stir well. Shape meat mixture into a 9- x 5-inch loaf; place on a rack in a broiler pan coated with cooking spray. Combine chili sauce and water; brush over loaf. Bake, uncovered, at 350° for 1 hour or until a meat thermometer inserted in center of loaf registers 160°. Let stand 10 minutes before slicing. Yield: 10 servings.

 TIP: Use leftovers to make satisfying meat loaf sandwiches for lunch or dinner.

Stuffed Peppers

6 medium-size green peppers (about 2 pounds)
¾ pound ground round
1¾ cups finely chopped onion (about 1 large)
1 clove garlic, minced
1 (29-ounce) can tomato sauce
1½ cups cooked rice
1 teaspoon dried marjoram
1 teaspoon dried oregano
⅛ teaspoon salt
¼ teaspoon pepper
¼ cup plus 2 tablespoons nonfat sour cream

1. Cut tops off peppers. Remove and discard seeds and membranes. Finely chop pepper tops, discarding stems; set chopped pepper aside. Cook pepper cups in boiling water to cover 5 minutes. Drain peppers; set aside.

2. Cook chopped green pepper, ground round, onion, and garlic in a Dutch oven over medium-high heat 5 minutes, stirring until meat crumbles and vegetables are tender. Add tomato sauce and next 5 ingredients. Bring to a boil; reduce heat and simmer, uncovered, 6 minutes, stirring often.

3. Spoon meat mixture evenly into pepper cups; place in an 11- x 7-inch baking dish. Add hot water to dish to depth of ½ inch. Bake, uncovered, at 350° for 20 to 25 minutes or until thoroughly heated. Spoon 1 tablespoon sour cream on each pepper before serving. Yield: 6 servings.

 FOR A QUICK MEAL: Serve with warm breadsticks and sliced apples.

POINTS:
4

EXCHANGES:
1½ Starch
2 Vegetable
1 Lean Meat

PER SERVING:
Calories 234
Carbohydrate 33.6g
Fat 3.9g (saturated 1.2g)
Fiber 5.6g
Protein 18.0g
Cholesterol 33mg
Sodium 962mg
Calcium 72mg
Iron 4.7mg

Shepherd's Pie

POINTS:
7

EXCHANGES:
4 Starch
2 Lean Meat

PER SERVING:
Calories 387
Carbohydrate 59.0g
Fat 6.2g (saturated 1.9g)
Fiber 4.2g
Protein 25.3g
Cholesterol 45mg
Sodium 666mg
Calcium 112mg
Iron 3.2mg

2½ pounds baking potatoes, peeled and cut into eighths
1½ cups fat-free milk, divided
¼ cup fat-free egg substitute
2 tablespoons yogurt-based spread (such as Brummel & Brown)
1 teaspoon salt, divided
1 teaspoon pepper, divided
Cooking spray
1½ cups finely chopped onion
2 cloves garlic, minced
1 pound ground round
1 teaspoon dried sage
½ teaspoon ground thyme
¼ cup all-purpose flour
1 (15¼-ounce) can white corn, drained

1. Place potato in a medium saucepan; add water to cover. Bring to a boil. Cover, reduce heat, and simmer 15 minutes or until potato is tender; drain.

2. Combine potato, ½ cup milk, egg substitute, spread, ½ teaspoon salt, and ½ teaspoon pepper in a large bowl. Beat at medium speed of an electric mixer 1 to 2 minutes or until fluffy. Set aside.

3. Coat a large nonstick skillet with cooking spray; place skillet over medium-high heat until hot. Add onion and garlic; cook 3 minutes, stirring constantly. Add ground round, sage, thyme, and remaining ½ teaspoon salt and ½ teaspoon pepper. Cook 5 minutes, stirring until meat crumbles and is browned. Combine remaining 1 cup milk and flour, and add to meat mixture. Let simmer, uncovered, 10 minutes, stirring occasionally.

4. Pour meat mixture into an 11- x 7-inch baking dish. Sprinkle with corn, and cover with mashed potatoes. Bake, uncovered, at 350° for 30 minutes or until bubbly. Let stand 10 minutes before serving. Yield: 6 (1-cup) servings.

Beef Fajitas

¾   pound lean beef flank steak
1½ tablespoons chili powder
½   teaspoon salt
Cooking spray
1   medium-size sweet red or green pepper, thinly sliced
    (about 1 cup)
1   medium onion, sliced and separated into rings
    (about 1½ cups)
2   tablespoons lime juice
6   (8-inch) fat-free flour tortillas
1   medium tomato, chopped (about ¾ cup)
⅓   cup minced fresh cilantro
2   cups shredded romaine lettuce
½   cup chunky salsa (optional)
½   cup nonfat sour cream (optional)

POINTS:

5

EXCHANGES:

1½ Starch
1½ Vegetable
1 Medium-Fat Meat

PER SERVING:

Calories 241
Carbohydrate 31.3g
Fat 6.0g (saturated 2.4g)
Fiber 3.2g
Protein 15.6g
Cholesterol 28mg
Sodium 601mg
Calcium 25mg
Iron 3.3mg

1. Cut steak diagonally across grain into ¼-inch-thick slices. Toss steak with chili powder and salt; set aside.

2. Coat a large nonstick skillet with cooking spray; place over medium-high heat until hot. Add pepper and onion; cook 4 minutes or until crisp-tender. Remove from skillet, and set aside.

3. Add steak to skillet, and cook 2 to 3 minutes or until steak is done. Stir in lime juice.

4. Wrap tortillas in wax paper; microwave at HIGH 30 seconds. Divide steak evenly among warm tortillas. Top each with pepper and onion mixture, tomato, cilantro, and lettuce; roll up tortillas. If desired, serve with salsa and sour cream. Yield: 6 servings.

FOR A QUICK MEAL: Serve with fat-free refried beans topped with reduced-fat Monterey Jack cheese and offer cubed fresh melon for dessert.

Hungarian Goulash

POINTS:
6

EXCHANGES:
1½ Starch
2 Vegetable
3 Lean Meat

PER SERVING:
Calories 319
Carbohydrate 32.9g
Fat 7.6g (saturated 2.0g)
Fiber 3.2g
Protein 29.1g
Cholesterol 73mg
Sodium 816mg
Calcium 61mg
Iron 5.0mg

1   tablespoon olive oil
1   pound lean boneless top sirloin steak, cut into ½-inch cubes
1½ cups cubed portobello mushrooms (about 1 mushroom cap)
1   large onion, cut into thin wedges
1   medium-size green pepper, chopped (about 1 cup)
4   cloves garlic, minced
2   (14.5-ounce) cans beef broth, divided
1   tablespoon all-purpose flour
1   (14.5-ounce) can no-salt-added diced tomatoes, undrained
¼   cup dry red wine
1   teaspoon unsweetened cocoa
1   teaspoon sweet Hungarian paprika
3   cups hot cooked egg noodles (cooked without salt or fat)
¼   cup plus 2 tablespoons nonfat sour cream

1. Heat oil in a Dutch oven over medium-high heat 1 minute; add steak. Cook 3 minutes or until lightly browned, stirring often. Add mushrooms, onion, green pepper, and garlic. Cook 5 minutes or until vegetables are tender, stirring often.

2. Combine ¼ cup beef broth and flour; stirring with a whisk until smooth. Stir into steak mixture; add remaining broth, tomatoes, and wine, stirring well. Bring to a boil. Cover, reduce heat, and simmer 30 minutes. Add cocoa and paprika. Cook, uncovered, 20 minutes or until steak is tender, stirring occasionally.

3. Divide noodles among 6 serving bowls. Spoon steak mixture over noodles. Top each serving with 1 tablespoon sour cream. Yield: 6 servings (½ cup noodles and 1 cup steak mixture per serving).

Beef Stroganoff

Cooking spray
1 pound lean boneless top sirloin steak, cut into ½-inch cubes
½ cup chopped onion
1 cup coarsely chopped fresh mushrooms
1 tablespoon all-purpose flour
½ cup dry white wine
1 cup beef broth
½ teaspoon dried thyme
¼ teaspoon salt
¼ teaspoon pepper
½ cup 66%-less-fat sour cream (such as Land O'Lakes)
4 cups hot cooked egg noodles (cooked without salt or fat)

POINTS:
9

EXCHANGES:
3 Starch
4 Lean Meat

PER SERVING:
Calories 438
Carbohydrate 47.8g
Fat 9.9g (saturated 3.6g)
Fiber 4.2g
Protein 36.1g
Cholesterol 127mg
Sodium 555mg
Calcium 102mg
Iron 6.6mg

1. Coat a large nonstick skillet with cooking spray; place over medium-high heat until hot. Add steak and onion, and cook 3 to 5 minutes or until steak is browned, stirring constantly. Add mushrooms; cook 2 minutes, stirring often. Add flour; cook, stirring constantly, 1 minute. Stir in wine, and simmer 2 minutes. Add broth and next 3 ingredients; simmer, uncovered, 7 to 10 minutes or until reduced by half.

2. Remove skillet from heat; stir in sour cream. To serve, place 1 cup noodles on each serving plate; spoon beef mixture evenly over noodles. Yield: 4 servings (1 cup noodles and ½ cup meat mixture per serving).

FOR A QUICK MEAL: Serve with steamed broccoli and for dessert, Coconut Cream Pie (page 49).

Steak au Poivre (photo, page 100)

POINTS:
5

EXCHANGES:
½ Starch
3½ Lean Meat

PER SERVING:
Calories 225
Carbohydrate 6.9g
Fat 9.0g (saturated 3.8g)
Fiber 0.8g
Protein 27.3g
Cholesterol 75mg
Sodium 681mg
Calcium 73mg
Iron 4.4mg

1   tablespoon cracked black pepper
2   (4-ounce) beef tenderloin steaks (1 inch thick)
Cooking spray
¼   cup brandy
½   cup beef broth
¼   teaspoon salt
¼   teaspoon sugar
3   tablespoons 66%-less-fat sour cream (such as Land
       O'Lakes)

1. Press cracked black pepper evenly onto both sides of steaks.

2. Coat a large nonstick skillet with cooking spray; place skillet over medium-high heat until hot. Add steaks, and cook 5 minutes on each side or to desired degree of doneness. Transfer to a serving platter; set aside, and keep warm.

3. Add brandy to skillet; let simmer 30 seconds or until liquid is reduced to a glaze. Add beef broth, salt, and sugar. Simmer, uncovered, 4 to 5 minutes or until liquid is reduced by half.

4. Remove skillet from heat; stir in sour cream. Serve with steak. Yield: 2 servings (1 steak and 2 tablespoons sauce per serving).

 FOR A QUICK MEAL: Serve with Dijon Scalloped Potatoes (page 181) and glazed baby carrots.

Sunday Pot Roast

1   (2-pound) lean boneless bottom round roast
3   cloves garlic, sliced
½   teaspoon freshly ground pepper
Cooking spray
1   (14.5-ounce) can beef broth
½   cup dry red wine
1   large onion, sliced
18   small round red potatoes, halved (about 1½ pounds)
18   baby carrots (about ½ pound)

1. Trim fat from roast. Make slits in top of roast. Insert a garlic slice into each slit. Rub roast with pepper. Brown roast on all sides over medium-high heat in an ovenproof Dutch oven coated with cooking spray.

2. Add beef broth, wine, and onion. Cover and bake at 325° for 2 hours. Add potato and carrot. Cover and bake 1 to 1½ hours or until roast and vegetables are tender. Yield: 6 servings (3 ounces roast, 3 potatoes, 3 carrots, and ¼ cup gravy per serving).

COOKING SECRET: Slow and gentle cooking is the key to making this lean roast tender and delicious.

POINTS:
6

EXCHANGES:
1½ Starch
1 Vegetable
4 Very Lean Meat

PER SERVING:
Calories 311
Carbohydrate 27.9g
Fat 5.6g (saturated 2.0g)
Fiber 3.6g
Protein 36.3g
Cholesterol 74mg
Sodium 469mg
Calcium 47mg
Iron 4.9mg

Veal Parmigiana (photo, page 99)

POINTS:
6

EXCHANGES:
1 Starch
3½ Lean Meat

PER SERVING:
Calories 260
Carbohydrate 16.4g
Fat 8.5g (saturated 2.5g)
Fiber 2.0g
Protein 28.6g
Cholesterol 98mg
Sodium 761mg
Calcium 102mg
Iron 2.1mg

1   (14.5-ounce) can diced tomatoes, undrained
¼   cup dry red wine
1   tablespoon minced fresh basil
1   tablespoon minced fresh thyme
½   cup Italian-seasoned breadcrumbs
1   tablespoon water
1   egg white
1   pound veal scaloppine or very thin veal cutlets (¼ inch thick)
Cooking spray
1   tablespoon vegetable oil, divided
¼   cup (1 ounce) shredded part-skim mozzarella cheese

1. Combine first 4 ingredients in a medium saucepan; bring to a boil. Reduce heat, and simmer, uncovered, 3 minutes or until slightly thickened. Set aside.

2. Place breadcrumbs in a shallow dish. Combine water and egg white; beat lightly. Dip veal into egg white mixture, turning to coat; dredge in breadcrumbs.

3. Coat a large nonstick skillet with cooking spray; add 1½ teaspoons oil. Place over medium-high heat until hot. Add half of veal cutlets to skillet; cook 1 to 2 minutes on each side or until lightly browned. Remove veal from skillet, and keep warm. Recoat skillet with cooking spray, and add remaining 1½ teaspoons oil. Repeat procedure with remaining veal cutlets.

4. Return all veal to skillet; pour tomato mixture over veal. Sprinkle cheese over tomato mixture. Cover and cook 3 minutes or until cheese melts. Yield: 4 servings.

 FOR A QUICK MEAL: Serve with crisp breadsticks and angel hair pasta tossed with fresh herbs.

Lemon-Herb Lamb Chops

4 (5-ounce) lean lamb loin chops
1 teaspoon dried rosemary
1 teaspoon dried sage
1 teaspoon grated lemon rind
¼ teaspoon salt
¼ teaspoon pepper
Cooking spray

1. Trim fat from chops. Combine rosemary and next 4 ingredients in a small bowl. Rub herb mixture on both sides of chops. Coat grill rack with cooking spray; place on grill over medium coals (300° to 350°). Place chops on rack; grill, covered, about 8 to 10 minutes per side or to desired degree of doneness. Yield: 4 servings.

 FOR A QUICK MEAL: Serve with rice pilaf, steamed mixed vegetables, and Red and Gold Fruit Salad (page 131).

POINTS:
4

EXCHANGES:
3½ Lean Meat

PER SERVING:
Calories 187
Carbohydrate 0.4g
Fat 8.5g (saturated 3.0g)
Fiber 0.2g
Protein 25.6g
Cholesterol 81mg
Sodium 218mg
Calcium 24mg
Iron 1.9mg

Braised Lamb with (photo, facing page) Lemon and Rosemary Beans

POINTS:
6

EXCHANGES:
3 Starch
2½ Lean Meat

PER SERVING:
Calories 340
Carbohydrate 42.8g
Fat 7.2g (saturated 2.5g)
Fiber 7.3g
Protein 26.9g
Cholesterol 44mg
Sodium 390mg
Calcium 129mg
Iron 6.1mg

2 cups dried cannellini beans
2½ pounds lamb shanks
Cooking spray
1 medium onion, chopped (about 1 cup)
1 medium carrot, chopped (about ¾ cup)
½ cup dry white wine
6 cups water
3 sprigs fresh thyme
1 sprig fresh rosemary
1 tablespoon chopped fresh rosemary
1 teaspoon salt
½ teaspoon pepper
3 cloves garlic, minced
3 tablespoons fresh lemon juice

1. Sort and wash beans; drain well, and set aside.

2. Place a 6-quart ovenproof Dutch oven over medium heat until hot. Coat lamb shanks with cooking spray; add to pan, and cook 12 minutes or until brown on all sides, turning often. Remove shanks from pan; set aside, and keep warm.

3. Add onion and carrot to pan; cook 5 minutes, stirring constantly. Add wine; bring to a boil, stirring constantly. Reduce heat, and simmer, uncovered, 2 minutes. Add beans, lamb shanks, water, thyme, and rosemary sprig. Bring to a boil. Transfer to oven, and bake, covered, at 350° for 2 hours or until beans are done and meat is tender. Stir in chopped rosemary and next 3 ingredients. Cover and bake 30 additional minutes.

4. Remove meat from bones, and return to pan; stir in lemon juice. Cook over medium-high heat until slightly thickened. Serve immediately. Yield: 7 (1-cup) servings.

Country-Style Pork Chops
(recipe, page 102)

Veal Parmigiana
(recipe, page 94)

Steak au Poivre
(recipe, page 92)

Fennel Roasted Pork

1	(¾-pound) pork tenderloin
1	teaspoon fennel seeds, crushed
¼	teaspoon salt
¼	teaspoon pepper
Cooking spray	
⅔	cup chopped Granny Smith apple (about ½ of a small apple)
⅓	cup apple juice
¼	cup sliced leeks or green onions
¼	cup apple juice
2	teaspoons cornstarch

POINTS:

3

EXCHANGES:

½ Fruit

2½ Very Lean Meat

PER SERVING:

Calories 136

Carbohydrate 9.5g

Fat 2.5g (saturated 0.8g)

Fiber 0.8g

Protein 18.1g

Cholesterol 55mg

Sodium 191mg

Calcium 20mg

Iron 1.5mg

1. Trim fat from tenderloin. Combine fennel seeds, salt, and pepper. Rub mixture on all sides of pork tenderloin.

2. Coat grill rack with cooking spray. Light gas grill on one side; let grill preheat 10 to 15 minutes. Place tenderloin on rack opposite hot lava rocks; grill, covered, 25 minutes or until a meat thermometer inserted into thickest part of tenderloin registers 160°.

3. While meat cooks, combine apple, ⅓ cup apple juice, and leeks. Bring to a boil; cover, reduce heat, and simmer 5 minutes. Combine ¼ cup apple juice and cornstarch; stir well. Add cornstarch mixture to leek mixture. Bring to a boil; reduce heat and simmer, stirring constantly, 1 minute or until thickened.

4. Thinly slice pork. Serve with apple and leek mixture. Yield: 4 servings.

COOKING SECRET: If you don't have a mortar and pestle, use any rounded kitchen tool you have to crush fennel seeds. A bowl and the handle of an ice cream scoop work nicely.

Country-Style Pork Chops (photo, page 98)

POINTS:
6

EXCHANGES:
1 Starch
3½ Lean Meat

PER SERVING:
Calories 275
Carbohydrate 14.7g
Fat 10.3g (saturated 3.2g)
Fiber 0.5g
Protein 28.3g
Cholesterol 68mg
Sodium 564mg
Calcium 73mg
Iron 2.0mg

¼ cup fat-free egg substitute
1 teaspoon water
¼ cup plus 2 tablespoons all-purpose flour, divided
2 tablespoons fine, dry breadcrumbs
½ teaspoon paprika
¼ teaspoon ground sage
½ teaspoon salt, divided
½ teaspoon pepper, divided
¼ teaspoon garlic powder
4 (6-ounce) lean center-cut pork loin chops (½ inch thick), trimmed
2 teaspoons vegetable oil
Cooking spray
½ cup one-third-less-salt chicken broth (such as Swanson's Natural Goodness)
¾ cup fat-free milk, divided

1. Combine egg substitute and water in a shallow dish. Combine 2 tablespoons flour, breadcrumbs, paprika, sage, ¼ teaspoon salt, ¼ teaspoon pepper, and garlic powder in a large heavy-duty, zip-top plastic bag. Dip chops, two at a time, into egg substitute mixture; place in plastic bag with flour mixture. Seal bag, and shake until chops are coated; repeat with remaining chops.

2. Heat oil in a large nonstick skillet coated with cooking spray; add chops. Cook 2 minutes on each side or until browned. Add broth; bring to a boil. Cover, reduce heat, and simmer 15 minutes or until meat is tender. Transfer chops to a serving platter, reserving liquid in skillet, and keep warm.

3. Combine remaining ¼ cup flour and ¼ cup milk, stirring until smooth; stir flour mixture into liquid in skillet with a whisk. Gradually stir in remaining ½ cup milk, remaining ¼ teaspoon salt, and remaining ¼ teaspoon pepper; bring just to a simmer. Cook until thickened, stirring constantly; spoon sauce over chops. Yield: 4 servings (1 pork chop and ¼ cup sauce per serving).

Currant Glazed Pork Chops

2   tablespoons red currant jelly

1½ tablespoons ketchup

1½ teaspoons white vinegar

Dash of ground cinnamon

Dash of ground cloves

4   (4-ounce) boneless center-cut pork loin chops (½ inch thick)

¼   teaspoon pepper

⅛   teaspoon salt

Cooking spray

POINTS:
5

EXCHANGES:
½ Starch
3½ Lean Meat

PER SERVING:
Calories 214
Carbohydrate 8.4g
Fat 8.3g (saturated 2.8g)
Fiber 0.2g
Protein 25.1g
Cholesterol 71mg
Sodium 218mg
Calcium 9mg
Iron 1.0mg

1. Combine first 5 ingredients in a small saucepan. Cook over medium heat until jelly melts, stirring constantly.

2. Sprinkle both sides of pork with pepper and salt. Coat grill rack with cooking spray; place on grill over medium-hot coals (350° to 400°). Place pork on rack; brush with jelly mixture. Grill, covered, 5 minutes on each side or until done, basting frequently with jelly mixture. Yield: 4 servings.

FOR A QUICK MEAL: Serve with roasted new potatoes, green beans, and Strawberry Shortcake (page 55).

Peach Sauced Ham

POINTS:

5

EXCHANGES:

1 Starch

1 Fruit

2½ Very Lean Meat

PER SERVING:

Calories 243

Carbohydrate 27.0g

Fat 6.0g (saturated 1.6g)

Fiber 0.4g

Protein 20.7g

Cholesterol 56mg

Sodium 1015mg

Calcium 16mg

Iron 1.6mg

½   cup peach all-fruit spread
2   tablespoons sliced green onions
2   tablespoons orange juice
1   tablespoon Dijon mustard
2   teaspoons Worcestershire sauce
½   cup canned, chopped peaches in juice, drained, or 1
        medium-size fresh peach, peeled and chopped
1   (1-pound) reduced-fat, lower-salt ham steak
Cooking spray

1. Combine first 5 ingredients in a small bowl; stir with a whisk. Reserve half of fruit spread mixture. Place remaining mixture in a small saucepan. Stir in peaches. Bring just to a boil, stirring constantly. Set aside, and keep warm.

2. Trim fat from ham steak. Coat grill rack with cooking spray; place on grill over medium-hot coals (350° to 400°). Place ham on rack; grill, covered, 9 to 11 minutes or until thoroughly heated, turning occasionally, and basting with reserved fruit spread mixture. Cut into 4 pieces. Remove ham to a serving platter. Spoon peach sauce over ham. Yield: 4 servings.

 FOR A QUICK MEAL: Serve with baked sweet potatoes and green peas.

poultry

Chicken à la King

POINTS:

6

EXCHANGES:

2 Starch

3½ Very Lean Meat

½ Fat

PER SERVING:

Calories 309

Carbohydrate 32.2g

Fat 6.7g (saturated 2.6g)

Fiber 4.0g

Protein 32.2g

Cholesterol 88mg

Sodium 920mg

Calcium 126mg

Iron 3.1mg

1   cup chopped, cooked chicken breast
¼   cup fat-free milk
¼   cup frozen English peas, thawed
¼   teaspoon pepper
1   (10¾-ounce) can reduced-fat, reduced-sodium cream of
    chicken soup, undiluted (such as Campbell's Healthy
    Request)
1   (7-ounce) can sliced mushrooms, drained
1   (2-ounce) jar diced pimiento, drained
2   tablespoons 66%-less-fat sour cream (such as Land
    O'Lakes)
2   slices reduced-calorie whole wheat bread, toasted
Paprika

1. Combine first 7 ingredients in a large saucepan; cook over low heat 10 minutes, stirring often. Remove from heat. Stir in sour cream.

2. Cut each slice of toast in half diagonally, if desired, and place on serving plates. Spoon 1¼ cups chicken mixture evenly over each serving of toast. Sprinkle with paprika. Yield: 2 servings (1 slice toast and 1¼ cups chicken mixture per serving).

TIP: Keep chopped, cooked chicken breast in the freezer so that you can easily assemble quick entrées like this one. For tender chunks of chicken every time, place 4 (4-ounce) skinned, boned chicken breast halves on a baking sheet coated with cooking spray. Sprinkle the chicken with ¼ teaspoon each salt and pepper. Bake at 350° for 25 minutes. Cool slightly and chop. You'll have 4 servings, or about 3 cups, chopped, cooked chicken.

Chicken and Broccoli Cannelloni

1   (8-ounce) package cannelloni, uncooked
3   cups fat-free milk
⅓   cup all-purpose flour
⅛   teaspoon ground nutmeg
¼   teaspoon salt, divided
¼   teaspoon pepper
¾   cup freshly grated Romano cheese
2   cups finely chopped, cooked chicken breast
1   (10-ounce) package frozen chopped broccoli, thawed, drained, and squeezed dry
2   cloves garlic, minced
½   teaspoon dried Italian seasoning
1   (26-ounce) jar fire-roasted tomato and garlic pasta sauce (such as Classico)

POINTS:

6

EXCHANGES:

2½ Starch
1 Vegetable
2½ Very Lean Meat
½ Fat

PER SERVING:

Calories 326
Carbohydrate 42.0g
Fat 5.1g (saturated 1.8g)
Fiber 3.7g
Protein 26.5g
Cholesterol 47mg
Sodium 598mg
Calcium 249mg
Iron 3.0mg

1. Cook cannelloni according to package directions, omitting salt and fat; drain. Rinse under cold water; drain and set aside.

2. Combine milk, flour, nutmeg, ⅛ teaspoon salt, and pepper in a medium saucepan; stir well with a whisk. Bring to a boil; reduce heat, and simmer, uncovered, 5 minutes or until thickened and bubbly, stirring constantly. Remove from heat; stir in cheese, and set white sauce aside.

3. Combine chicken, broccoli, garlic, Italian seasoning, remaining ⅛ teaspoon salt, and 1 cup white sauce in a large bowl. Let cool.

4. Spoon 1 cup pasta sauce into a 13- x 9-inch baking dish. Spoon chicken mixture evenly into cooked cannelloni, and arrange in dish. Pour remaining pasta sauce over stuffed cannelloni; pour remaining white sauce on top. Bake, uncovered, at 350° for 35 minutes or until bubbly. Let stand 10 minutes before serving. Yield: 7 servings.

FOR A QUICK MEAL: Serve with thin Italian breadsticks, a mixed greens salad drizzled with fat-free Italian dressing, and for dessert, raspberry sorbet.

Chicken Tetrazzini

POINTS:

6

EXCHANGES:

3 Starch

2½ Very Lean Meat

PER SERVING:

Calories 315

Carbohydrate 41.3g

Fat 3.7g (saturated 1.3g)

Fiber 1.7g

Protein 26.5g

Cholesterol 48mg

Sodium 305mg

Calcium 174mg

Iron 2.9mg

Cooking spray

8 ounces spaghetti, uncooked

1 (14½-ounce) can one-third-less salt chicken broth (such as Swanson's Natural Goodness)

½ (8-ounce) package sliced fresh mushrooms

½ cup chopped green pepper

⅓ cup chopped onion

1 cup fat-free evaporated milk

⅓ cup all-purpose flour

¼ teaspoon pepper

⅛ teaspoon ground nutmeg

2 cups chopped, cooked chicken breast

2 tablespoons dry sherry or fat-free evaporated milk

¼ cup freshly grated Parmesan cheese

1. Coat an 8-inch square baking dish with cooking spray; set aside. Cook spaghetti according to package directions, omitting salt and fat. Drain and set aside.

2. Combine broth and next 3 ingredients in a large saucepan. Bring to a boil; cover, reduce heat, and simmer 5 minutes or until vegetables are tender. Combine evaporated milk and next 3 ingredients in a small bowl, stirring well with a whisk. Add to vegetable mixture. Cook over medium heat until mixture is thickened and bubbly, stirring constantly. Add chicken and sherry.

3. Toss cooked spaghetti with chicken mixture. Spoon into prepared baking dish. Sprinkle with Parmesan cheese. Bake, uncovered, at 400° for 10 minutes or until golden. Yield: 6 (1-cup) servings.

 TIME-SAVING TIP: Keep preparation time to a minimum for this creamy entrée by using rotisserie chicken.

Chicken and Dumplings

3   (10½-ounce) cans low-sodium chicken broth (such as
      Campbell's)
1   cup thinly sliced carrot
1   cup thinly sliced celery
½   cup chopped onion
½   teaspoon dried thyme
½   teaspoon dried rosemary, crushed
¼   teaspoon salt
¼   teaspoon pepper
1   pound skinned, boned chicken breast halves, cut into cubes
1⅓ cups all-purpose flour
1¼ teaspoons baking powder
¼   teaspoon salt
½   cup plus 1 tablespoon fat-free milk
2   tablespoons reduced-calorie margarine, melted

POINTS:
7

EXCHANGES:
3 Starch
3 Lean Meat

PER SERVING:
Calories 361
Carbohydrate 42.4g
Fat 7.1g (saturated 2.0g)
Fiber 3.1g
Protein 31.3g
Cholesterol 64mg
Sodium 698mg
Calcium 173mg
Iron 4.6mg

1. Combine first 8 ingredients in a Dutch oven; bring to a boil.
Add chicken; cover, reduce heat, and simmer 10 minutes.

2. Combine flour, baking powder, and ¼ teaspoon salt. Add milk
and margarine, stirring to form a stiff dough. Drop dough by
heaping tablespoonfuls on top of broth mixture to create 8
dumplings. Cover, reduce heat, and simmer 15 minutes or until
dumplings are done. Ladle chicken mixture into 4 bowls; top each
serving with dumplings. Yield: 4 servings (1 cup chicken mixture
and 2 dumplings per serving).

 COOKING SECRET: It's easier to cube raw chicken if you
freeze it just until it's firm.

Chicken Pot Pie (photo, page 119)

POINTS:
6

EXCHANGES:
2 Starch
1 Vegetable
2½ Very Lean Meat
½ Fat

PER SERVING:
Calories 293
Carbohydrate 35.0g
Fat 5.3g (saturated 1.6g)
Fiber 2.3g
Protein 25.2g
Cholesterol 85mg
Sodium 883mg
Calcium 156mg
Iron 1.8mg

1   (10¾-ounce) can reduced-fat, reduced-sodium cream of
       mushroom soup, undiluted
½   cup fat-free milk
½   teaspoon salt
¼   teaspoon pepper
3   cups chopped, cooked chicken breast
2   cups frozen peas and carrots, thawed
½   cup chopped onion
½   cup thinly sliced celery
1   (2-ounce) jar sliced pimiento, drained
1½ cups reduced-fat biscuit and baking mix (such as Bisquick)
¾   cup fat-free milk
1   egg
Butter-flavored cooking spray (such as I Can't Believe
       It's Not Butter)
1   tablespoon freshly grated Parmesan cheese

1. Combine soup and next 3 ingredients in saucepan; bring to a boil. Reduce heat, and simmer, uncovered, 1 minute, stirring constantly until smooth.

2. Add chicken, peas and carrots, and next 3 ingredients to soup mixture, stirring well. Bring to a boil; cover, reduce heat, and simmer 5 minutes. Pour mixture into an 11- x 7-inch baking dish.

3. Combine biscuit and baking mix, ¾ cup milk, and egg; stir until smooth. Spread evenly over chicken mixture; coat with cooking spray. Sprinkle with cheese. Bake, uncovered, at 375° for 30 to 35 minutes or until golden. Yield: 6 servings.

TIP: For individual pot pies, pour 1 cup chicken mixture into 6 (8-ounce) ramekins, and top with ¾ cup crust mixture. Spray each with butter-flavored cooking spray, and sprinkle with ½ teaspoon Parmesan cheese. Bake, uncovered, at 375° for 30 to 35 minutes or until golden.

Orange Chicken Stir-Fry

⅔ cup orange juice

⅓ cup low-sodium soy sauce

⅓ cup dry sherry

1 tablespoon plus 1 teaspoon cornstarch

½ teaspoon dried crushed red pepper

Cooking spray

4 green onions, cut into 1-inch pieces

1 cup baby carrots, cut lengthwise into quarters

3 cups broccoli flowerets

2 teaspoons vegetable oil

1 pound skinned, boned chicken breast halves, cut into 1½-inch pieces

1 tablespoon peeled, grated gingerroot

3 cloves garlic, minced

1 (8-ounce) can sliced water chestnuts, drained

2 cups hot cooked brown rice (cooked without salt or fat)

POINTS:

7

EXCHANGES:

2½ Starch

2½ Vegetable

3 Very Lean Meat

PER SERVING:

Calories 381

Carbohydrate 49.8g

Fat 5.2g (saturated 1.0g)

Fiber 4.4g

Protein 33.2g

Cholesterol 66mg

Sodium 768mg

Calcium 91mg

Iron 2.8mg

1. Combine first 5 ingredients, stirring well. Set aside.

2. Coat a large nonstick skillet or wok with cooking spray; place over medium-high heat until hot. Add green onions and carrot; stir-fry 2 minutes. Add broccoli; stir-fry 3 minutes or until vegetables are crisp-tender. Remove vegetables from skillet.

3. Add oil to skillet; place over medium-high heat until hot. Add chicken, gingerroot, and garlic; stir-fry 8 minutes or until chicken is done. Add orange juice mixture to skillet; cook until sauce is thickened and bubbly. Return vegetables to skillet; stir in water chestnuts. Cook until thoroughly heated. Serve over rice. Yield: 4 servings (½ cup rice and 1½ cups chicken mixture per serving).

 FOR A QUICK MEAL: Fresh orange slices and a cluster of red grapes complement this one-dish meal.

Chicken Cacciatore

POINTS:
8

EXCHANGES:
3 Starch
2 Vegetable
3 Very Lean Meat

PER SERVING:
Calories 400
Carbohydrate 55.4g
Fat 3.8g (saturated 0.6g)
Fiber 3.9g
Protein 35.4g
Cholesterol 66mg
Sodium 408mg
Calcium 41mg
Iron 3.8mg

Cooking spray
1½ pounds skinned, boned chicken breast halves, cut into large
    pieces
1½ cups sliced fresh mushrooms
1 cup chopped onion
2 (15-ounce) cans chunky tomato sauce (such as Hunt's
    Ready Sauce with Onions, Celery, and Green Bell
    Peppers)
½ cup dry white wine
1½ teaspoons dried Italian seasoning
⅛ teaspoon pepper
12 ounces spaghetti, uncooked

1. Coat a large skillet with cooking spray; place over medium-high heat until hot. Add chicken; brown on all sides. Remove chicken from skillet.

2. Add mushrooms and onion to skillet; cook 2 minutes, stirring constantly. Add chicken, tomato sauce, and next 3 ingredients; bring to a boil. Cover, reduce heat, and simmer 15 minutes or until chicken is done.

3. Meanwhile, cook spaghetti according to package directions, omitting salt and fat. Drain. Serve chicken and sauce over spaghetti. Yield: 6 servings (1 cup spaghetti and 1 cup chicken mixture per serving).

 FOR A QUICK MEAL: Serve with a spinach salad and crusty French bread.

Chicken Fingers with Horseradish Dipping Sauce

1 cup crushed corn flakes cereal
½ teaspoon paprika
¼ teaspoon dried thyme
¼ teaspoon salt
¼ teaspoon pepper
⅓ cup low-fat buttermilk
1 pound chicken tenders
Cooking spray
Horseradish Dipping Sauce

1. Combine first 5 ingredients in a heavy-duty, zip-top plastic bag. Pour buttermilk into a shallow dish; dip chicken into buttermilk. Transfer chicken to plastic bag; seal bag, and shake until chicken is coated.

2. Place chicken on a jelly-roll pan coated with cooking spray. Coat strips lightly with cooking spray. Bake, uncovered, at 400° for 19 minutes or until chicken is done. Serve with Horseradish Dipping Sauce. Yield: 6 servings.

Horseradish Dipping Sauce

¾ cup nonfat sour cream
¼ cup reduced-calorie mayonnaise
2 tablespoons prepared horseradish
2 tablespoons grated onion
⅛ teaspoon salt

1. Combine all ingredients in a small bowl. Serve with chicken fingers. Yield: 1⅓ cups (about 3½ tablespoons per serving).

FOR A QUICK MEAL: Serve with reduced-fat potato chips and for dessert, Buttermilk Brownies with Chocolate-Mint Glaze (page 58).

POINTS:
4

EXCHANGES:
1 Starch
2½ Very Lean Meat

PER SERVING:
Calories 185
Carbohydrate 14.1g
Fat 3.9g (saturated 0.8g)
Fiber 0.4g
Protein 21.1g
Cholesterol 48mg
Sodium 462mg
Calcium 106mg
Iron 1.4mg

Chicken Piccata

POINTS:

5

EXCHANGES:

½ Starch

3½ Very Lean Meat

½ Fat

PER SERVING:

Calories 213

Carbohydrate 10.4g

Fat 6.1g (saturated 0.9g)

Fiber 0.4g

Protein 27.4g

Cholesterol 66mg

Sodium 456mg

Calcium 16mg

Iron 1.4mg

½   cup one-third-less salt chicken broth (such as Swanson's Natural Goodness)

3   tablespoons fresh lemon juice

1   teaspoon cornstarch

½   teaspoon grated lemon rind

½   teaspoon sugar

⅛   teaspoon garlic powder

4   (4-ounce) skinned, boned chicken breast halves

⅓   cup all-purpose flour

½   teaspoon salt

¼   teaspoon pepper

1   tablespoon olive oil

2   teaspoons reduced-calorie margarine

Chopped fresh parsley (optional)

1. Combine first 6 ingredients in a small bowl; set aside.

2. Place chicken between 2 sheets of heavy-duty plastic wrap; flatten to ¼-inch thickness, using a meat mallet or rolling pin. Cut each breast into 2-inch pieces.

3. Combine flour, salt, and pepper in a small bowl. Dredge chicken pieces in flour mixture. Heat oil in a large nonstick skillet over medium heat. Add chicken; cook 4 minutes on each side or until done. Remove chicken from skillet. Set aside; keep warm.

4. Stir broth mixture, and add to skillet. Cook over medium heat until mixture is thickened and bubbly, stirring constantly. Stir in margarine. Spoon sauce over chicken; sprinkle with parsley, if desired. Yield: 4 servings.

 FOR A QUICK MEAL: Serve with parslied noodles and Lemony Strawberry-Spinach Salad (page 130).

PREP: 8 minutes COOK: 1 hour and 18 minutes

Cassoulet

Cooking spray
1 pound skinned, boned chicken breast halves, cut into cubes
1 medium onion, chopped
1 large carrot, coarsely chopped
2 stalks celery, coarsely chopped
2 tablespoons tomato paste
½ cup dry white wine
3 (15.8-ounce) cans Great Northern beans, rinsed and drained
1 (14½-ounce) can one-third-less salt chicken broth (such as Swanson's Natural Goodness)
3 sprigs fresh marjoram or ½ teaspoon dried oregano
7 ounces smoked turkey sausage, sliced

POINTS:
6

EXCHANGES:
2½ Starch
4 Very Lean Meat

PER SERVING:
Calories 329
Carbohydrate 37.1g
Fat 4.6g (saturated 1.4g)
Fiber 6.5g
Protein 34.6g
Cholesterol 64mg
Sodium 798mg
Calcium 120mg
Iron 4.3mg

1. Coat a large ovenproof Dutch oven with cooking spray; place over medium-high heat until hot. Cook chicken 2 minutes or until browned. Remove from pan; set aside.

2. Add onion, carrot, and celery to Dutch oven. Cook 5 minutes or until browned, stirring often. Add tomato paste. Cook, stirring constantly, 1 minute. Add wine; simmer 2 minutes. Add beans, broth, and marjoram; bring to a boil. Add reserved chicken and sausage.

3. Cover and bake at 350° for 45 minutes. Let stand 15 minutes before serving. Yield: 6 (1½-cup) servings.

NOTE: A cassoulet is a classic French dish consisting of white beans and various meats. It is traditionally covered and cooked slowly to blend the flavors.

Easy Barbecued Chicken (photo, facing page)

POINTS:

4

EXCHANGES:

1 Starch

4 Very Lean Meat

PER SERVING:

Calories 203

Carbohydrate 16.3g

Fat 3.7g (saturated 1.0g)

Fiber 0.8g

Protein 29.2g

Cholesterol 78mg

Sodium 451mg

Calcium 24mg

Iron 1.3mg

½   cup ketchup

2   tablespoons finely chopped onion

2   tablespoons peach or apricot jam

2   tablespoons white vinegar

1   teaspoon Worcestershire sauce

1½ teaspoons chili powder

⅛   teaspoon garlic powder

Cooking spray

4   (6-ounce) skinned, bone-in chicken breast halves

1. Combine first 7 ingredients in a small saucepan; bring to a boil. Reduce heat, and simmer, uncovered, 5 minutes. Set aside ½ cup sauce; keep warm.

2. Coat grill rack with cooking spray; place on grill over medium-hot coals (350° to 400°). Place chicken, bone side up, on rack; grill, covered, 8 minutes on each side or until done, turning once and basting with remaining barbecue sauce. Serve with reserved ½ cup barbecue sauce. Yield: 4 servings (1 chicken breast and 2 tablespoons sauce per serving).

FOR A QUICK MEAL: Serve with Garden Potato Salad (page 136) and for dessert, Blackberry Cobbler (page 51) with a dollop of Vanilla Ice Cream (page 47).

Red Beans and Rice
(recipe, page 125)

Chicken Pot Pie
(recipe, page 110)

Lemon-Herb Roasted Chicken
(recipe, page 123)

Coq au Vin

Cooking spray

4 (6-ounce) skinned, bone-in chicken breast halves

1½ cups small fresh mushroom halves

16 pearl onions, peeled

1 cup sliced carrot

1 cup dry red wine

1 teaspoon dried parsley flakes

½ teaspoon chicken bouillon granules

½ teaspoon dried marjoram

½ teaspoon dried thyme

¼ teaspoon salt

⅛ teaspoon garlic powder

⅛ teaspoon pepper

1 bay leaf

2 tablespoons all-purpose flour

3 tablespoons cold water

2 slices turkey bacon, cooked and crumbled

POINTS:

5

EXCHANGES:

2 Vegetable

4 Lean Meat

PER SERVING:

Calories 264

Carbohydrate 12.9g

Fat 7.4g (saturated 1.9g)

Fiber 2.0g

Protein 34.2g

Cholesterol 96mg

Sodium 693mg

Calcium 55mg

Iron 2.6mg

1. Coat a large skillet with cooking spray; place over medium-high heat until hot. Add chicken; brown on all sides. Remove from pan; keep warm.

2. Add mushrooms, onions, and carrot to skillet; cook 2 minutes. Add wine and next 8 ingredients. Add reserved chicken. Bring to a boil; cover, reduce heat, and simmer 15 to 20 minutes or until chicken is done. Transfer chicken to a serving platter; keep warm. Remove and discard bay leaf from skillet.

3. Combine flour and water, stirring with a whisk. Add to liquid in skillet. Bring to a boil; cook 3 minutes or until thickened, stirring constantly. Spoon over chicken. Sprinkle with bacon. Yield: 4 servings (1 chicken breast and ¼ cup sauce per serving).

Oven-Fried Chicken

POINTS:

5

EXCHANGES:

2 Starch

2 Very Lean Meat

PER SERVING:

Calories 255

Carbohydrate 33.1g

Fat 2.8g (saturated 0.7g)

Fiber 0.6g

Protein 22.3g

Cholesterol 57mg

Sodium 753mg

Calcium 17mg

Iron 3.4mg

3 egg whites, lightly beaten
2 tablespoons water
2 cups crushed corn flakes cereal
1 teaspoon dried sage
¾ teaspoon paprika
½ teaspoon salt
½ teaspoon pepper
½ teaspoon dried thyme
1 (3-pound) broiler-fryer, skinned and cut up
Cooking spray

1. Beat egg whites and water in a shallow dish with a whisk. Combine crushed cereal and next 5 ingredients in a shallow dish. Dip chicken in egg mixture; dredge in cereal mixture. Place chicken, bone side down, in a jelly-roll pan coated with cooking spray. Coat chicken pieces with cooking spray. Bake, uncovered, at 450° for 45 minutes or until done. Yield: 6 servings.

 FOR A QUICK MEAL: Serve with Hearty Mashed Potatoes (page 179) and Buttermilk Biscuits (page 31).

Lemon-Herb Roasted Chicken (photo, page 120)

1   (3-pound) roasting chicken
3   sprigs fresh rosemary, thyme, or sage
2   tablespoons chopped fresh rosemary, thyme, or sage
1   teaspoon grated lemon rind
3   tablespoons fresh lemon juice
¼   teaspoon salt
¼   teaspoon pepper
2   cloves garlic, minced

1. Remove and discard giblets from chicken. Rinse chicken under cold water; pat dry. Trim excess fat. Starting at neck cavity, loosen skin from breast and drumsticks by inserting fingers, gently pushing between skin and meat.

2. Place fresh rosemary, thyme, or sage sprigs under loosened skin over breast. Combine chopped rosemary and remaining 5 ingredients; brush over chicken and in cavity of chicken.

3. Place chicken on a rack in roasting pan. Insert meat thermometer into meaty part of thigh, making sure not to touch bone.

4. Bake, uncovered, at 400° for 1 hour or until thermometer registers 180°. Let stand 15 minutes before serving. Yield: 6 servings.

FOR A QUICK MEAL: Serve with steamed vegetables and hot cooked rice that has been tossed with lemon zest and chopped fresh herbs.

POINTS:
2

EXCHANGES:
2½ Very Lean Meat

PER SERVING:
Calories 105
Carbohydrate 1.8g
Fat 2.7g (saturated 0.7g)
Fiber 0.5g
Protein 17.6g
Cholesterol 57mg
Sodium 161mg
Calcium 27mg
Iron 1.1mg

Roasted Cornish Hen and Peaches

POINTS:

8

EXCHANGES:

2 Fruit

3½ Lean Meat

PER SERVING:

Calories 344

Carbohydrate 32.8g

Fat 12.6g (saturated 5.8g)

Fiber 1.9g

Protein 24.7g

Cholesterol 46mg

Sodium 371mg

Calcium 15mg

Iron 2.4mg

1 (1¼-pound) Cornish hen
1 tablespoon lemon juice
¼ teaspoon salt
⅛ teaspoon pepper
1 (15-ounce) can peach halves in extra-light syrup (such as Del Monte Lite)
¼ teaspoon ground ginger
1 tablespoon brown sugar
1 teaspoon cornstarch

1. Remove and discard skin and giblets from hen. Rinse hen under cold water, and pat dry. Split hen in half lengthwise. Place hen halves, cut side down, in a shallow roasting pan. Brush with lemon juice. Sprinkle with salt and pepper. Bake, uncovered, at 425° for 20 minutes.

2. Drain peaches, reserving syrup. Arrange peaches around hen in roasting pan. Stir ginger into syrup; pour syrup mixture into pan around hen. Bake, uncovered, 20 additional minutes or until hen halves are done.

3. Combine brown sugar and cornstarch in a small saucepan; stir well. Transfer hen and peaches to serving platter. Pour juices from pan into a glass measure. Add water to make ½ cup; gradually stir into sugar mixture in saucepan. Cook over medium heat, stirring constantly, until mixture is thickened and bubbly. Cook 1 additional minute. Pour sauce over hen and peaches. Serve immediately. Yield: 2 servings (1 hen half, about 1 cup peach halves, and ¼ cup sauce per serving).

 FOR A QUICK MEAL: Serve with herbed rice pilaf and steamed green beans.

Red Beans and Rice (photo, page 118)

1 family-size bag quick-cooking boil-in-bag rice, uncooked
1 slice turkey bacon, diced
1 large onion, minced
4 cloves garlic, minced
1 (16-ounce) can red kidney beans, rinsed and drained
1 (14.5-ounce) can no-salt-added stewed tomatoes, undrained
4 ounces low-fat smoked turkey sausage, cut into
     bite-size pieces
1 teaspoon hot sauce
½ teaspoon freshly ground pepper
2 bay leaves

1. Cook rice according to package directions, omitting salt
and fat.

2. While rice cooks, cook bacon in a 3-quart saucepan over medium heat until browned. Add onion and garlic; cook until crisp-
tender, stirring often. Stir in beans and remaining 5 ingredients.
Bring to a boil; cover, reduce heat, and simmer 20 minutes, stirring occasionally.

3. Remove and discard bay leaves. Spoon rice into individual
bowls; top evenly with bean mixture. Yield: 4 servings (1 cup rice
and 1 cup bean mixture per serving).

> **FOR A QUICK MEAL:** Serve with crusty French bread, and
> for dessert, Double Cherry Crisp (page 52).

POINTS:
7

EXCHANGES:
4½ Starch
1 Vegetable
½ High-Fat Meat

PER SERVING:
Calories 409
Carbohydrate 74.4g
Fat 4.8g (saturated 1.3g)
Fiber 8.3g
Protein 15.5g
Cholesterol 26mg
Sodium 601mg
Calcium 91mg
Iron 4.0mg

PREP: 7 minutes COOK: 15 minutes

Spaghetti with Italian Turkey Sausage

POINTS:

9

EXCHANGES:

3½ Starch

1 Vegetable

2 Medium-Fat Meat

PER SERVING:

Calories 444

Carbohydrate 58.6g

Fat 11.3g (saturated 3.7g)

Fiber 5.3g

Protein 27.6g

Cholesterol 73mg

Sodium 961mg

Calcium 163mg

Iron 5.6mg

¾ pound sweet Italian turkey sausage (about 3 links)
1 cup chopped onion
2 cloves garlic, minced
1 (14.5-ounce) can diced tomatoes with basil, garlic, and oregano
1 cup low-sodium chicken broth (such as Campbell's)
½ cup tomato paste
2 teaspoons dried Italian seasoning
8 ounces spaghetti, uncooked
¼ cup grated Parmesan cheese

1. Remove casings from sausage. Cook sausage in a large nonstick skillet over medium-high heat until sausage is browned, stirring until it crumbles. Add onion and garlic; cook 5 minutes or until onion is tender, stirring often. Stir in tomatoes and next 3 ingredients; bring just to a boil. Reduce heat, and simmer, uncovered, 5 minutes, stirring occasionally.

2. While sauce simmers, cook spaghetti according to package directions, omitting salt and fat; drain. Place spaghetti in a serving dish; top with sauce. Sprinkle with cheese. Yield: 4 servings (1 cup spaghetti, 1 cup sauce, and 1 tablespoon cheese per serving).

FOR A QUICK MEAL: Pick up a 10-ounce package of Italian-style salad greens and some French rolls at the supermarket to complete your meal.

salads

Caesar Salad

POINTS:
1

EXCHANGES:
1 Vegetable
½ Fat

PER SERVING:
Calories 49
Carbohydrate 3.2g
Fat 3.2g (saturated 0.6g)
Fiber 0.7g
Protein 1.3g
Cholesterol 1mg
Sodium 119mg
Calcium 26mg
Iron 0.4mg

¼   cup water
3   tablespoons white wine vinegar
2   tablespoons olive oil
1   tablespoon Dijon mustard
1   teaspoon Worcestershire sauce
½   teaspoon garlic pepper seasoning (such as Lawry's)
2   cloves garlic, crushed
10 cups torn romaine lettuce
1   cup fat-free Caesar croutons
2   tablespoons freshly shredded Parmesan cheese
Freshly ground pepper

1. Combine first 7 ingredients in a small bowl; stir well with a whisk.

2. Combine lettuce and dressing in a large bowl; toss well. Add croutons and cheese; toss well. Sprinkle with pepper. Yield: 10 (1-cup) servings.

TIME-SAVING TIP: Buy 2 (10-ounce) packages torn romaine lettuce, available in the produce section of your grocery store, to keep preparation time to a minimum.

Greek Salad Bowl (photo, page 137)

1 (14-ounce) can quartered artichoke hearts, drained
1 cup sliced cucumber
⅓ cup crumbled feta cheese
12 kalamata olives
1 large tomato, cut into thin wedges
⅓ cup fresh lemon juice
1 tablespoon olive oil
½ teaspoon dried oregano
½ teaspoon lemon-pepper seasoning
1 clove garlic, crushed
Freshly ground pepper

1. Combine first 5 ingredients in a large bowl. Combine lemon juice and next 4 ingredients in a small bowl; stir with a whisk until blended. Pour over vegetable mixture; toss to coat. Sprinkle with pepper. Yield: 6 (¾-cup) servings.

TIP: If your cucumber is large, slice it in half lengthwise, and then cut crosswise into thin slices.

POINTS:
2

EXCHANGES:
2 Vegetable
1 Fat

PER SERVING:
Calories 97
Carbohydrate 10.2g
Fat 5.9g (saturated 1.3g)
Fiber 2.0g
Protein 3.1g
Cholesterol 6mg
Sodium 236mg
Calcium 63mg
Iron 1.1mg

Lemony Strawberry-Spinach Salad (photo, page 4)

POINTS:
1

EXCHANGES:
2 Vegetable
½ Fat

PER SERVING:
Calories 75
Carbohydrate 12.9g
Fat 2.6g (saturated 0.5g)
Fiber 3.1g
Protein 1.8g
Cholesterol 0mg
Sodium 38mg
Calcium 58mg
Iron 1.6mg

1   (10-ounce) package trimmed fresh spinach, torn
2   cups sliced fresh strawberries
½   cup thinly sliced purple onion
⅓   cup fresh lemon juice
3   tablespoons sugar
1   tablespoon vegetable oil
2   teaspoons grated lemon rind
Freshly ground pepper

1. Combine first 3 ingredients in a large bowl.

2. Combine lemon juice, sugar, and oil in a small bowl; stir with a whisk until blended. Stir in lemon rind. Pour over spinach mixture; toss. Sprinkle with pepper. Yield: 6 (2-cup) servings.

TIP: A light, lemony vinaigrette adds a refreshing twist to this traditional strawberry-spinach salad.

Red and Gold Fruit Salad

2 tablespoons fresh lemon juice

1 tablespoon honey

¼ teaspoon ground ginger

⅛ teaspoon ground cardamom

2 cups fresh cantaloupe balls

2 nectarines, cut into very thin wedges (about 2 cups)

1 pint fresh raspberries

1. Combine first 4 ingredients in a bowl; stir well. Add melon balls, nectarine, and raspberries, tossing gently to coat. Cover and chill 1 hour. Yield: 6 (1-cup) servings.

TIP: Look for cantaloupes that are heavy for their size. This means they'll be extra sweet and juicy. A nectarine is ripe when its smooth skin is deep gold with a red blush.

POINTS:

1

EXCHANGES:

1½ Fruit

PER SERVING:

Calories 84

Carbohydrate 20.4g

Fat 0.7g (saturated 0.1g)

Fiber 4.9g

Protein 1.4g

Cholesterol 0mg

Sodium 5mg

Calcium 19mg

Iron 0.5mg

Waldorf Salad

POINTS:
1

EXCHANGE:
1 Fruit

PER SERVING:
Calories 63
Carbohydrate 15.2g
Fat 0.5g (saturated 0.2g)
Fiber 1.8g
Protein 1.0g
Cholesterol 1mg
Sodium 15mg
Calcium 33mg
Iron 0.2mg

1½ cups coarsely chopped apple (about 1 medium)
1   cup coarsely chopped pear (about 1 medium)
1   cup red seedless grapes
½   cup thinly sliced celery
⅓   cup vanilla nonfat yogurt
1   tablespoon unsweetened apple juice
¼   teaspoon ground ginger

1. Combine first 4 ingredients in a medium bowl. Combine yogurt, apple juice, and ginger; pour over apple mixture, tossing to coat. Yield: 6 (⅔-cup) servings.

TIP: Ground ginger gives a sweet, peppery flavor to this traditional salad.

Frozen Cranberry Salad

1   cup finely chopped fresh cranberries
3   tablespoons sugar
1   (15-ounce) can apricot halves in juice, undrained
1   (8-ounce) carton light process raspberry-flavored cream
        cheese
1   tablespoon fresh orange juice
1   cup finely chopped fresh pear (about 1 medium)
2   teaspoons grated orange rind
2   cups fat-free frozen whipped topping, thawed
9   lettuce leaves

POINTS:

3

EXCHANGES:

1 Starch
½ Fruit
½ Fat

PER SERVING:

Calories 133
Carbohydrate 22.7g
Fat 3.6g (saturated 2.3g)
Fiber 0.9g
Protein 2.8g
Cholesterol 12mg
Sodium 109mg
Calcium 35mg
Iron 0.2mg

1. Combine cranberries and sugar; let stand 10 minutes. Drain apricots well, reserving ⅓ cup juice; finely chop apricots.

2. Combine reserved apricot juice, cream cheese, and orange juice in a medium mixing bowl; beat at medium speed of an electric mixer until fluffy. Stir in cranberry mixture, apricot, pear, and orange rind; fold in whipped topping.

3. Spoon mixture into a 9-inch square pan. Cover and freeze 8 hours or until firm. Cut into individual squares, and serve on lettuce leaves. Yield: 9 servings (1 square per serving).

TIP: This classic salad is ideal for a brunch or luncheon. Dress it up with a dollop of nonfat sour cream and fresh mint sprigs, if desired.

Marinated Bean Salad

POINTS:
1

EXCHANGES:
1½ Starch

PER SERVING:
Calories 121
Carbohydrate 25.0g
Fat 0.5g (saturated 0.1g)
Fiber 7.5g
Protein 5.9g
Cholesterol 0mg
Sodium 480mg
Calcium 59mg
Iron 2.1mg

½   pound fresh green beans, trimmed and cut into 1-inch pieces (about 2 cups)
1   (16-ounce) can dark red kidney beans, rinsed and drained
½   cup thinly sliced celery
½   cup chopped sweet red pepper
1   small onion, thinly sliced (about 1 cup)
⅓   cup balsamic vinaigrette
1   teaspoon freshly ground pepper
½   teaspoon dried tarragon
¼   teaspoon salt

1. Cook green beans in boiling water to cover 5 minutes or until crisp-tender; drain. Plunge into cold water to stop the cooking process; drain well.

2. Combine green beans, kidney beans, and next 3 ingredients in a large bowl. Combine vinaigrette and remaining 3 ingredients; stir well with a whisk. Pour vinaigrette mixture over vegetables; toss gently to coat. Cover and marinate in refrigerator at least 2 hours. Yield: 4 (1½-cup) servings.

COOKING SECRET: If fresh green beans aren't available, substitute 2 cups frozen cut green beans that have been cooked until crisp-tender.

Crunchy Coleslaw

3   cups packaged finely shredded green cabbage
¾   cup packaged preshredded carrot
½   cup chopped onion
¼   cup finely chopped sweet red pepper
½   cup plain nonfat yogurt
1   tablespoon honey-Dijon mustard
½   teaspoon salt
¼   teaspoon pepper

1. Combine first 4 ingredients in a medium bowl; toss well. Combine yogurt and remaining 3 ingredients; pour over cabbage mixture. Toss gently to coat. Cover and chill 1 hour. Stir just before serving. Yield: 6 (½-cup) servings.

TIME-SAVING TIP: Buy preshredded green cabbage and carrot, available in the produce section of your grocery store, to keep preparation time to a minimum.

POINTS:
0

EXCHANGE:
1 Vegetable

PER SERVING:
Calories 34
Carbohydrate 6.6g
Fat 0.3g (saturated 0.0g)
Fiber 1.4g
Protein 1.8g
Cholesterol 0mg
Sodium 269mg
Calcium 59mg
Iron 0.4mg

Garden Potato Salad

POINTS:
2

EXCHANGES:
1 Starch
1 Vegetable

PER SERVING:
Calories 111
Carbohydrate 21.1g
Fat 1.6g (saturated 0.3g)
Fiber 2.7g
Protein 4.0g
Cholesterol 2mg
Sodium 255mg
Calcium 47mg
Iron 1.2mg

3   medium-size round red potatoes (about 1 pound)
1   cup frozen cut green beans
1   cup frozen whole-kernel corn
⅓   cup chopped sweet red pepper
⅓   cup thinly sliced green onions
½   cup nonfat sour cream
2   tablespoons reduced-fat mayonnaise
½   teaspoon salt
½   teaspoon pepper
½   teaspoon dried oregano
¼   teaspoon ground cumin

1. Peel potatoes, and cut into cubes. Place potato in saucepan; add water to cover. Bring to a boil; cover, reduce heat, and simmer, 15 minutes or until tender. Drain and let cool.

2. Place green beans and corn in a saucepan; add water to cover. Bring to a boil; cover, reduce heat, and simmer, 5 minutes or until beans are crisp-tender. Drain and let cool.

3. Combine potato, green beans and corn, red pepper, and green onions in a bowl. Combine sour cream and remaining 5 ingredients; stir well. Pour sour cream mixture over potato mixture and toss well. Cover and chill 2 hours. Yield: 6 (⅔-cup) servings.

 FOR A QUICK MEAL: Serve with Easy Barbecued Chicken (page 116) or Oven-Fried Chicken (page 122).

Greek Salad Bowl
(recipe, page 129)

Cajun Catfish Sandwiches
(recipe, page 149)

138

Chicken Tenders Salad
(recipe, page 142)

Grilled Cheese
Sandwiches Deluxe
(recipe, page 148)

Fresh Tomato Soup
(recipe, page 164)

Curried Chicken Salad

¼ cup plain nonfat yogurt
¼ cup reduced-fat mayonnaise
¾ to 1 teaspoon curry powder
¼ teaspoon bottled minced ginger
⅛ teaspoon salt
1 rotisserie chicken, meat removed and chopped (about 2 cups)
1 cup packaged preshredded carrot
½ cup chopped green onions
¼ cup raisins, coarsely chopped
Leaf lettuce

POINTS:

6

EXCHANGES:

1 Fruit
3 Lean Meat
1 Fat

PER SERVING:

Calories 262
Carbohydrate 15.8g
Fat 12.9g (saturated 2.7g)
Fiber 1.7g
Protein 22.8g
Cholesterol 98mg
Sodium 887mg
Calcium 61mg
Iron 2.0mg

1. Combine first 5 ingredients in a small bowl; stir well. Add chicken and next 3 ingredients; stir to coat. Serve over lettuce leaves. Yield: 3 servings (1 cup chicken mixture per serving).

FOR A QUICK MEAL: Serve with a fresh fruit bowl of cubed cantaloupe and red grapes.

Chicken Tenders Salad (photo, page 139)

POINTS:
7

EXCHANGES:
2 Starch
2 Vegetable
4 Very Lean Meat
½ Fat

PER SERVING:
Calories 382
Carbohydrate 40.9g
Fat 7.8g (saturated 2.1g)
Fiber 4.3g
Protein 37.7g
Cholesterol 71mg
Sodium 945mg
Calcium 223mg
Iron 4.7mg

¼ cup all-purpose flour
½ teaspoon pepper
1 pound chicken tenders
3 tablespoons fat-free egg substitute
⅓ cup fat-free milk
1 cup Italian-seasoned breadcrumbs
3 tablespoons sesame seeds
Cooking spray
1 (10-ounce) package romaine lettuce, torn
2 large tomatoes, cut into wedges
½ purple onion, sliced (about 1½ cups)
¼ cup (1 ounce) shredded reduced-fat Cheddar cheese
Reduced-fat salad dressing

1. Combine flour and pepper in a large heavy-duty zip-top plastic bag. Add chicken tenders; seal bag, and shake to coat.

2. Combine egg substitute and milk in a shallow dish, stirring well. Combine breadcrumbs and sesame seeds in a shallow dish.

3. Dip each chicken tender in egg mixture, and dredge in breadcrumb mixture. Place in a single layer on a baking sheet coated with cooking spray. Coat chicken tenders with cooking spray. Bake, uncovered, at 425° for 20 minutes or until done. Cut chicken tenders diagonally into 1-inch pieces.

4. Place 2 cups lettuce on 4 individual serving plates. Divide chicken, tomato, and onion evenly among plates. Top each serving with 1 tablespoon cheese. Serve with salad dressing (salad dressing not included in analysis). Yield: 4 servings.

sandwiches

Tuna Salad Sandwiches

POINTS:
6

EXCHANGES:
2 Starch
2 Lean Meat
½ Fat

PER SERVING:
Calories 283
Carbohydrate 29.9g
Fat 9.1g (saturated 1.6g)
Fiber 3.6g
Protein 20.6g
Cholesterol 30mg
Sodium 664mg
Calcium 90mg
Iron 2.6mg

2   (6-ounce) cans chunk white tuna in water, drained and flaked
¾   cup diced celery
½   cup minced onion
⅓   cup reduced-fat mayonnaise
2   tablespoons minced fresh parsley
2   tablespoons drained and chopped roasted red pepper
2   tablespoons lemon juice
⅛   teaspoon ground white pepper
8   (1-ounce) slices whole wheat bread
8   leaves romaine lettuce

1. Combine first 8 ingredients in a medium bowl; stir well.

2. Spread tuna mixture evenly on 4 bread slices. Top each with 2 leaves lettuce and remaining bread slices. Yield: 4 servings.

COOKING SECRET: Pimiento can be substituted for the roasted red peppers in this quick and easy sandwich.

Italian-Style Hoagies

2 ounces thinly sliced Italian roast beef (4 slices)

2 ounces thinly sliced peppered ham (4 slices)

4 (¾-ounce) slices reduced-fat provolone cheese or part-skim mozzarella cheese

4 leaves romaine lettuce

8 thin slices tomato

4 thin slices onion, separated into rings

4 (3-ounce) whole wheat submarine rolls, split

4 pepperoncini peppers, sliced

2 teaspoons dried oregano

1½ tablespoons red wine vinegar

2 teaspoons fat-free Italian dressing

1. Layer first 6 ingredients evenly onto bottom halves of rolls. Top with peppers and oregano.

2. Combine vinegar and dressing; drizzle evenly over meat and vegetables. Cover with tops of rolls. Yield: 4 servings.

TIP: Ask your grocer's deli department for very thin slices of the Italian roast beef and peppered ham for this stacked sandwich.

POINTS:

7

EXCHANGES:

3 Starch

1 Vegetable

1½ Medium-Fat Meat

PER SERVING:

Calories 331

Carbohydrate 49.4g

Fat 7.6g (saturated 2.6g)

Fiber 3.1g

Protein 21.3g

Cholesterol 23mg

Sodium 957mg

Calcium 434mg

Iron 3.7mg

Canadian BLTs

POINTS:
5

EXCHANGES:
2 Starch
1 Vegetable
1½ Medium-Fat Meat

PER SERVING:
Calories 276
Carbohydrate 33.9g
Fat 7.1g (saturated 2.3g)
Fiber 4.2g
Protein 17.9g
Cholesterol 32mg
Sodium 1226mg
Calcium 94mg
Iron 2.4mg

8   slices Canadian bacon
⅓   cup 66%-less-fat sour cream (such as Land O'Lakes)
1   tablespoon fat-free Italian dressing
8   (1-ounce) slices rye bread, toasted
4   leaves romaine lettuce
8   (¼-inch) slices tomato
Freshly ground pepper

1. Cook bacon in a nonstick skillet over medium heat 4 minutes or until lightly browned.

2. Combine sour cream and Italian dressing in a small bowl; stir well. Spread evenly on one side of each bread slice.

3. Layer bacon, lettuce, and tomato evenly on 4 bread slices. Season with pepper. Top with remaining bread slices. Yield: 4 servings.

FOR A QUICK MEAL: Serve with Creamy Bean with Bacon Soup (page 156) or a low-fat pasta salad.

Turkey-Avocado Sandwiches

1 tablespoon plus 1 teaspoon coarse-grained brown mustard
8 slices rye bread
8 leaves romaine lettuce
4 (¾-ounce) slices reduced-fat Swiss cheese
8 (1-ounce) slices smoked turkey breast
8 thin slices purple onion
8 slices tomato
1 avocado, peeled, seeded, and mashed (about ½ cup)
Freshly ground pepper

1. Spread 1 teaspoon mustard on one side of 4 bread slices. Top evenly with lettuce, cheese, turkey, onion, and tomato. Spread one side of each remaining bread slice evenly with mashed avocado; sprinkle with pepper. Place on top of sandwiches, avocado side down. Secure sandwiches with wooden picks, and cut in half. Yield: 4 servings.

COOKING SECRET: The avocado is actually a fruit, not a vegetable. The flesh browns quickly when cut, so slice avocados right before you plan to eat them, or rub the cut surface with a little lemon juice to prevent browning.

POINTS:

7

EXCHANGES:

2½ Starch
2 Lean Meat
1 Fat

PER SERVING:

Calories 352
Carbohydrate 37.7g
Fat 12.0g (saturated 3.4g)
Fiber 6.6g
Protein 24.3g
Cholesterol 42mg
Sodium 1225mg
Calcium 326mg
Iron 3.1mg

Grilled Cheese (photo, page 140) Sandwiches Deluxe

POINTS:

9

EXCHANGES:

3 Starch

1 Low-Fat Milk

1 Medium-Fat Meat

PER SERVING:

Calories 421

Carbohydrate 58.4g

Fat 10.3g (saturated 3.4g)

Fiber 2.3g

Protein 24.2g

Cholesterol 21mg

Sodium 1177mg

Calcium 279mg

Iron 3.2mg

1	cup 1% low-fat cottage cheese
½	cup (2 ounces) shredded reduced-fat sharp Cheddar cheese
4	slices lower-sodium bacon, cooked and crumbled
½	cup chopped green onions
1	tablespoon reduced-fat mayonnaise
2	teaspoons Dijon mustard
8	(½-inch) slices sourdough bread
12	(¼-inch) slices plum tomato (about 2 tomatoes)

Butter-flavored cooking spray (such as I Can't Believe It's Not Butter)

1. Place cottage cheese in container of an electric blender; cover and process 30 seconds or until smooth. Transfer to a small bowl; stir in Cheddar cheese and next 4 ingredients.

2. Spread cottage cheese mixture evenly over 4 bread slices; arrange tomato slices evenly over cottage cheese mixture. Top with remaining bread slices.

3. Coat a large nonstick skillet or griddle with cooking spray; place over medium heat until hot. Add sandwiches; spray each side with cooking spray, and cook 2 to 3 minutes on each side or until golden. Yield: 4 servings.

 FOR A QUICK MEAL: Serve with Fresh Tomato Soup (page 164) and celery sticks.

Cajun Catfish Sandwiches (photo, page 138)

¼ cup Italian-seasoned breadcrumbs
1 tablespoon Cajun seasoning
2 teaspoons dried parsley flakes
4 (4-ounce) farm-raised catfish fillets
3 tablespoons fresh lemon juice (about 1 lemon)
Cooking spray
½ cup 66%-less-fat sour cream (such as Land O'Lakes)
4 (2-ounce) Kaiser rolls or hamburger buns, toasted
4 leaves green leaf lettuce
¼ cup mild salsa

1. Combine first 3 ingredients in a small bowl. Dip fish in lemon juice, and dredge in breadcrumb mixture.

2. Coat a large nonstick skillet with cooking spray. Place over medium-high heat until hot. Add fillets, and cook 4 to 5 minutes on each side or until fish flakes easily when tested with a fork.

3. Spread sour cream evenly on bottom halves of rolls. Top evenly with lettuce, fish, and salsa; cover with tops of rolls. Yield: 4 servings.

 FOR A QUICK MEAL: Serve with Crunchy Coleslaw (page 135) and Carrot Cake (page 53).

POINTS:
8

EXCHANGES:
2½ Starch
3 Lean Meat

PER SERVING:
Calories 372
Carbohydrate 40.6g
Fat 9.2g (saturated 2.6g)
Fiber 2.0g
Protein 28.9g
Cholesterol 71mg
Sodium 1121mg
Calcium 179mg
Iron 3.7mg

Shrimp Melts

POINTS:
6

EXCHANGES:
2 Starch
3 Very Lean Meat
1 Fat

PER SERVING:
Calories 310
Carbohydrate 32.1g
Fat 7.6g (saturated 3.3g)
Fiber 2.6g
Protein 27.7g
Cholesterol 144mg
Sodium 822mg
Calcium 366mg
Iron 3.7mg

1 pound cooked, peeled small fresh shrimp
¾ cup minced onion
½ cup 66%-less-fat sour cream (such as Land O'Lakes)
1½ tablespoons fresh lemon juice (about ½ lemon)
½ teaspoon dried dillweed
½ teaspoon Worcestershire sauce
½ teaspoon prepared mustard
¼ teaspoon celery seeds
4 English muffins, split and lightly toasted
4 (¾-ounce) slices reduced-fat sharp Cheddar cheese, cut in
    half diagonally

1. Combine first 8 ingredients in a medium bowl; stir well.

2. Place muffin halves on a baking sheet. Spoon shrimp mixture onto muffin halves; broil 3 inches from heat 3 minutes. Top each muffin half with one-half slice cheese; broil 3 additional minutes or until cheese melts. Yield: 4 servings (2 muffin halves per serving).

TIME-SAVING TIP: Ask the seafood department at your local grocery store to steam your fresh shrimp to keep preparation time to a minimum.

Meatball Sandwiches

¾ pound ground round
½ cup fresh breadcrumbs
¼ cup minced fresh parsley
¼ cup minced fresh basil
⅛ teaspoon ground white pepper
4 cloves garlic, minced
1 small onion, minced
1 egg white
Cooking spray
1 (26-ounce) jar pasta sauce with Burgundy wine (such as Five Brothers)
6 unsliced hoagie rolls
¼ cup plus 2 tablespoons shredded part-skim mozzarella cheese, divided

POINTS:

6

EXCHANGES:

2½ Starch
2 Lean Meat
½ Fat

PER SERVING:

Calories 324
Carbohydrate 39.0g
Fat 8.8g (saturated 2.4g)
Fiber 4.7g
Protein 23.0g
Cholesterol 37mg
Sodium 794mg
Calcium 180mg
Iron 4.4mg

1. Combine first 8 ingredients in a large bowl; stir well. Shape into 24 (¾-inch) meatballs.

2. Coat a large nonstick skillet with cooking spray. Place over medium heat 1 minute. Add meatballs, and cook 15 to 20 minutes or until done (cook in two batches, if necessary).

3. Combine meatballs and pasta sauce in a medium saucepan. Place over low heat until sauce is warm, stirring often. Keep warm.

4. Hollow out center of each hoagie roll. Spoon 4 meatballs into each roll. Spoon sauce evenly over meatballs. Top each sandwich with 1 tablespoon part-skim mozzarella cheese. Yield: 6 servings.

 COOKING SECRET: Use the leftover bread from the rolls to make the fresh breadcrumbs.

Hot Browns

POINTS:
8

EXCHANGES:
2½ Starch
3 Lean Meat

PER SERVING:
Calories 354
Carbohydrate 34.7g
Fat 11.0g (saturated 3.2g)
Fiber 1.7g
Protein 28.8g
Cholesterol 51mg
Sodium 656mg
Calcium 209mg
Iron 2.7mg

2 tablespoons reduced-calorie margarine
2 tablespoons all-purpose flour
½ cup fat-free milk
½ cup one-third-less salt chicken broth (such as Swanson's Natural Goodness)
⅓ cup (1.3-ounces) shredded reduced-fat mild Cheddar cheese
⅛ teaspoon ground red pepper
4 (½-inch) slices sourdough bread, toasted
½ pound sliced cooked turkey or chicken breast
2 slices lower-sodium bacon, cooked, drained, and crumbled
4 (¼-inch) slices tomato
2 tablespoons freshly grated Parmesan cheese

1. Melt margarine in a small saucepan over low heat; add flour, stirring until smooth. Cook 1 minute, stirring constantly. Gradually add milk and broth; cook over medium heat, stirring constantly, until thick and bubbly. Add Cheddar cheese and pepper; stir until cheese melts. Remove from heat.

2. Place bread slices on a jelly-roll pan. Top evenly with turkey, cheese sauce, crumbled bacon, tomato, and Parmesan cheese. Broil 3 inches from heat 3 minutes or just until bubbly. Serve immediately. Yield: 4 servings.

 NOTE: The Hot Brown is a famous open-faced sandwich that was created at the Brown Hotel in Louisville, Kentucky.

Sausage and Pepper Sandwiches

1 (8-ounce) can no-salt-added tomato sauce
¼ cup dry red wine
2 cloves garlic, minced
¾ pound hot Italian turkey sausage (4 links)
Olive oil-flavored cooking spray
1 small onion, sliced and separated into rings
1 green pepper, thinly sliced
½ (8-ounce) package sliced fresh mushrooms
1 teaspoon dried oregano
4 hoagie rolls, split

1. Combine first 3 ingredients in a small saucepan. Bring to a simmer. Cover, and cook 1 minute. Keep warm.

2. Split sausage lengthwise to, but not through, other side. Gently remove casing. Coat a large skillet with cooking spray. Place over medium-high heat 1 minute. Add sausage. Cover, and cook 10 minutes, turning occasionally. Spoon off any liquid. Cook, uncovered, 5 additional minutes or until sausage is lightly browned. Remove sausage from skillet, and set aside.

3. Add onion, pepper, and mushrooms to skillet. Cook 8 minutes or until tender, stirring often. Sprinkle with oregano. Cook 4 additional minutes.

4. Place sausage on rolls. Spoon vegetable mixture evenly over sausage. Top with tomato sauce mixture. Yield: 4 servings.

 FOR A QUICK MEAL: Serve these sandwiches with baked potato chips and low-fat praline ice cream.

POINTS:
8

EXCHANGES:
3 Starch
1 Vegetable
2 Medium-Fat Meat

PER SERVING:
Calories 422
Carbohydrate 50.0g
Fat 10.5g (saturated 3.1g)
Fiber 5.3g
Protein 26.9g
Cholesterol 90mg
Sodium 1040mg
Calcium 188mg
Iron 7.0mg

Slim Turkey-Black Bean Burgers

POINTS:
8

EXCHANGES:
2 Starch
1 Vegetable
2½ Lean Meat

PER SERVING:
Calories 301
Carbohydrate 37.1g
Fat 9.2g (saturated 2.2g)
Fiber 7.3g
Protein 22.6g
Cholesterol 67mg
Sodium 460mg
Calcium 88mg
Iron 2.8mg

2 teaspoons olive oil
1½ pounds ground turkey or ground round
1½ cups finely chopped onion (about 1 medium)
¾ cup finely chopped green pepper (about 1 medium)
1 clove garlic, minced
2 (8-ounce) cans no-salt-added tomato sauce
1 (15-ounce) can black beans, rinsed and drained
1 tablespoon chili powder
1 tablespoon cider vinegar
1 tablespoon Dijon mustard
2 teaspoons Worcestershire sauce
2 teaspoons honey
Pinch of ground red pepper
8 reduced-calorie whole wheat hamburger buns

1. Heat oil in a large nonstick skillet over medium-high heat. Add turkey and next 3 ingredients; cook 10 minutes or until turkey is done and vegetables are tender, stirring until turkey crumbles.

2. Stir in tomato sauce and next 7 ingredients; simmer, uncovered, 10 minutes. Spoon turkey mixture evenly onto bottom halves of hamburger buns; top with remaining halves of buns. Yield: 8 servings (¾ cup turkey-black bean mixture and 1 bun per serving).

 FOR A QUICK MEAL: Serve with sliced tomatoes and cucumbers and fresh strawberries.

soups

PREP: 17 minutes COOK: 1 hour

Creamy Bean with Bacon Soup

POINTS:
4

EXCHANGES:
1½ Starch
1 Medium-Fat Meat

PER SERVING:
Calories 226
Carbohydrate 24.7g
Fat 5.6g (saturated 1.3g)
Fiber 6.4g
Protein 11.1g
Cholesterol 25mg
Sodium 856mg
Calcium 74mg
Iron 0.7mg

3   (16-ounce) cans navy beans, rinsed and drained
2   (14½-ounce) cans one-third-less salt chicken broth (such as Swanson's Natural Goodness)
½   cup finely chopped onion
⅓   cup chopped carrot (about 1 medium)
¼   cup chopped celery (about 1 rib)
5   slices turkey bacon, chopped
2   cloves garlic, minced
1   cup fat-free half-and-half
¼   teaspoon pepper
Nonfat sour cream (optional)

1. Combine first 7 ingredients in a large saucepan. Bring to a boil; reduce heat, and simmer, uncovered, 1 hour. Cool 10 minutes. Remove 4 cups soup from saucepan; puree in a blender or food processor in batches, if necessary. Return to saucepan. Stir in half-and-half and pepper.

2. To serve, ladle soup into individual serving bowls, and top each serving with 1 tablespoon nonfat sour cream, if desired. Yield: 7 (1-cup) servings.

FOR A QUICK MEAL: Serve with saltine crackers and orange slices.

Avgolemono
(recipe, page 168)

Yellow Squash Casserole
(recipe, page 184)

Mushroom Risotto
(recipe, page 188)

PREP: 7 minutes COOK: 36 minutes

French Onion Soup (photo, facing page)

1   teaspoon olive oil
2½ pounds sweet onions, sliced and separated into rings
2   (14½-ounce) cans 99% fat-free beef broth (such as
       Swanson's Natural Goodness)
2   teaspoons dry sherry
2   teaspoons low-sodium Worcestershire sauce
4   (½-inch-thick) slices French baguette
½   cup (2 ounces) shredded Gruyère or Swiss cheese
Freshly ground pepper (optional)

1. Heat oil in a Dutch oven over medium-high heat 1 minute.
Add onion. Cook 12 minutes or until softened and golden, stirring often.

2. Stir in broth; bring to a boil. Cover, reduce heat, and simmer
20 minutes. Stir in sherry and Worcestershire sauce.

3. Place bread slices on a baking sheet, and broil 5½ inches from
heat 1 minute or until lightly browned. Turn bread; sprinkle evenly with cheese. Broil 1 additional minute or until cheese melts.

4. To serve, ladle 1¾ cups soup into individual bowls. Top each
serving with a toasted bread slice, and sprinkle with freshly
ground pepper, if desired. Serve immediately. Yield: 4 (1¾-cup)
servings.

FOR A QUICK MEAL: Serve with Caesar Salad (page 128)
and low-fat vanilla ice cream topped with sliced fresh
strawberries.

POINTS:
5

EXCHANGES:
1 Starch
4 Vegetable
1 Fat

PER SERVING:
Calories 254
Carbohydrate 37.0g
Fat 6.9g (saturated 3.0g)
Fiber 5.4g
Protein 9.8g
Cholesterol 16mg
Sodium 287mg
Calcium 212mg
Iron 1.2mg

Split Pea Soup

POINTS:
4

EXCHANGES:
3 Starch
1 Very Lean Meat

PER SERVING:
Calories 252
Carbohydrate 43.7g
Fat 2.2g (saturated 0.3g)
Fiber 4.7g
Protein 16.6g
Cholesterol 4mg
Sodium 326mg
Calcium 66mg
Iron 3.5mg

1	tablespoon reduced-calorie margarine
1½	cups minced onion
⅔	cup diced carrots (about 2 medium)
½	cup diced celery (about 2 ribs)
3	cloves garlic, minced
8	cups water
1	(16-ounce) package dried split green peas, rinsed and drained
¾	cup peeled, diced baking potato (about 1 medium)
¼	cup minced fresh basil
2	tablespoons minced fresh oregano
¾	teaspoon salt
½	teaspoon pepper
2	slices reduced-fat, lower-salt ham, finely chopped

1. Heat margarine in a large Dutch oven over medium heat until margarine is melted; add onion and next 3 ingredients. Cook 10 minutes or until vegetables are tender, stirring constantly. Add water, split peas, and potato. Bring to a boil; cover, reduce heat, and simmer 1 hour or until peas are tender.

2. Stir in basil and remaining ingredients. Yield: 8 (1-cup) servings.

 FOR A QUICK MEAL: Serve this soup with fat-free croutons and sliced apples.

Loaded Potato Soup

2   large baking potatoes, peeled and cut into ¾-inch cubes (about 1⅓ pounds)

2   teaspoons reduced-calorie margarine

2   tablespoons all-purpose flour

2½ cups fat-free milk

¾   cup (3 ounces) shredded reduced-fat sharp Cheddar cheese, divided

⅓   cup chopped green onions, divided

3   slices lower-sodium bacon, cooked, crumbled, and divided

½   teaspoon salt

¼   teaspoon pepper

½   (8-ounce) carton nonfat sour cream

POINTS:

5

EXCHANGES:

2 Starch

½ High-Fat Meat

½ Low-Fat Milk

PER SERVING:

Calories 261

Carbohydrate 35.8g

Fat 6.7g (saturated 3.0g)

Fiber 2.1g

Protein 14.7g

Cholesterol 18mg

Sodium 526mg

Calcium 342mg

Iron 0.7mg

1. Place potato in a large saucepan, and add water to cover. Bring to a boil; cover, reduce heat to medium, and cook 20 minutes or until potato is tender. Drain and mash. Set aside.

2. Melt margarine in a Dutch oven over low heat; add flour, stirring until smooth. Cook 1 minute, stirring constantly. Gradually add milk; cook over medium heat, stirring constantly, until thickened and bubbly.

3. Stir in potato, ½ cup cheese, 2 tablespoons green onions, 2 tablespoons crumbled bacon, salt, and pepper; cook just until thoroughly heated (do not boil). Stir in sour cream.

4. To serve, ladle into individual serving bowls and top evenly with remaining cheese, green onions, and bacon. Yield: 5 (1-cup) servings.

FOR A QUICK MEAL: A simple green salad and sliced oranges are all you need to round out a meal featuring this hearty soup.

Fresh Tomato Soup (photo, page 140)

POINTS:

1

EXCHANGES:

3 Vegetable

PER SERVING:

Calories 66

Carbohydrate 13.9g

Fat 0.6g (saturated 0.1g)

Fiber 2.9g

Protein 2.2g

Cholesterol 0mg

Sodium 349mg

Calcium 30mg

Iron 1.3mg

1⅓ pounds fresh tomatoes (about 4 medium)
⅔ cup water
⅓ cup chopped onion
1¼ cups one-third-less salt chicken broth (such as Swanson's Natural Goodness)
1 (8-ounce) can no-salt-added tomato sauce
½ teaspoon sugar
¼ teaspoon salt
⅛ teaspoon pepper
1 tablespoon chopped fresh basil
1 teaspoon chopped fresh thyme

1. With a knife, make a shallow X on bottom of each tomato. Dip tomatoes into a large pot of boiling water to blanch 30 seconds or just until skins begin to crack. Plunge immediately into ice water. Remove from water, and pull skin away, using a sharp paring knife. Gently remove seeds, and chop tomato.

2. Combine water and onion in a large saucepan. Bring to a boil; reduce heat, and simmer, uncovered, 5 minutes. Stir in tomato, chicken broth, and next 4 ingredients. Bring to a boil; cover, reduce heat, and simmer 25 minutes.

3. Stir in basil and thyme. Simmer, uncovered, 5 minutes. Set aside; cool 10 minutes.

4. Process half of mixture in an electric blender until smooth. Repeat with remaining mixture. Return to saucepan. Cook 3 to 4 minutes or until thoroughly heated. Serve immediately. Yield: 4 (1-cup) servings.

 FOR A QUICK MEAL: Serve with Grilled Cheese Sandwiches Deluxe (page 148).

Southwestern Vegetable Soup (photo, page 2)

2 cups chopped onion

2 cloves garlic, minced

½ cup water

1 tablespoon ground cumin

1 tablespoon ground coriander

1 cup salsa

1 medium-size sweet red pepper, chopped (about ¾ cup)

1 medium-size green pepper, chopped (about ¾ cup)

2 (15-ounce) cans black beans, rinsed and drained

2 (14.5-ounce) cans stewed tomatoes, undrained

2 cups frozen whole-kernel corn

3 tablespoons chopped fresh cilantro

POINTS:

3

EXCHANGES:

2 Starch

2 Vegetable

PER SERVING:

Calories 194

Carbohydrate 39.3g

Fat 1.4g (saturated 0.2g)

Fiber 6.2g

Protein 10.1g

Cholesterol 0mg

Sodium 576mg

Calcium 86mg

Iron 3.7mg

1. Cook onion and garlic in water in a large Dutch oven over medium-high heat 3 to 5 minutes, stirring often. Add cumin and coriander; cook 1 minute, stirring constantly. Stir in salsa and peppers. Cover, reduce heat, and simmer 5 minutes, stirring occasionally.

2. Add black beans and tomatoes; cover and simmer 10 minutes. Add corn; cook 5 additional minutes. Stir in cilantro just before serving. Yield: 8 (1-cup) servings.

FOR A QUICK MEAL: Serve this main-dish soup with Jalapeño Cornbread (page 30).

PREP: 3 minutes COOK: 17 minutes

Minestrone

POINTS:

2

EXCHANGES:

1 Starch

2 Vegetable

PER SERVING:

Calories 143

Carbohydrate 23.9g

Fat 1.9g (saturated 0.5g)

Fiber 3.3g

Protein 6.2g

Cholesterol 1mg

Sodium 509mg

Calcium 67mg

Iron 1.9mg

2 teaspoons olive oil

2 cloves garlic, minced

3 (14½-ounce) cans one-third-less salt chicken broth (such as Swanson's Natural Goodness)

1 (16-ounce) package frozen Italian-style vegetables

1 (16-ounce) can pinto beans, rinsed and drained

1 (14.5-ounce) can diced Italian-style tomatoes, undrained

¾ cup (3 ounces) tubetti or other small tubular pasta

1½ teaspoons dried Italian seasoning

3 tablespoons plus 1 teaspoon freshly grated Parmesan cheese

1. Heat oil in a large saucepan over medium heat. Add garlic, and cook 1 minute or until lightly browned. Stir in chicken broth and next 5 ingredients. Bring to a boil; reduce heat, and simmer, uncovered, 15 minutes or until pasta is tender.

2. Ladle into individual serving bowls, and sprinkle each serving with 1 teaspoon Parmesan cheese. Yield: 10 (1-cup) servings.

 FOR A QUICK MEAL: Serve this classic Italian soup with Italian-Style Hoagies (page 145).

Vegetable-Beef Soup

2   teaspoons olive oil
¾   pound lean boneless top sirloin steak, cut into ½-inch cubes
1   cup finely chopped onion
1   clove garlic, minced
3   (14½-ounce) cans beef broth, undiluted
1   tablespoon Worcestershire sauce
1¾ cups cubed unpeeled baking potato (about 1 large)
1¼ cups diced carrot
1   cup frozen cut green beans
½   cup small elbow macaroni, uncooked
½   teaspoon freshly ground pepper

POINTS:
3

EXCHANGES:
1 Starch
2 Very Lean Meat

PER SERVING:
Calories 157
Carbohydrate 16.6g
Fat 3.0g (saturated 0.8g)
Fiber 2.1g
Protein 15.8g
Cholesterol 21mg
Sodium 792mg
Calcium 34mg
Iron 2.5mg

1. Heat oil in a Dutch oven over medium-high heat 1 minute. Add steak, onion, and garlic. Cook 8 minutes or until steak is browned and onion is tender, stirring often.

2. Stir in broth and Worcestershire sauce. Cover, reduce heat, and simmer 30 minutes.

3. Stir in potato, carrot, and green beans. Cover and cook 20 minutes or until potato and carrot are tender.

4. Stir in macaroni and pepper. Bring to a boil; cover, reduce heat to medium, and cook 10 additional minutes or until macaroni is done, stirring occasionally. Yield: 9 (1-cup) servings.

COOKING SECRET: It's easier to slice sirloin steak if you partially freeze it first.

Avgolemono (photo, page 157)

POINTS:

5

EXCHANGES:
1½ Starch
2 Lean Meat

PER SERVING:
Calories 229
Carbohydrate 23.1g
Fat 4.1g (saturated 1.1g)
Fiber 0.8g
Protein 20.8g
Cholesterol 103mg
Sodium 537mg
Calcium 36mg
Iron 2.0mg

½ teaspoon olive oil
½ cup finely chopped onion (about ½ small)
1 clove garlic, minced
2 (14½-ounce) cans one-third-less salt chicken broth (such as
    Swanson's Natural Goodness)
½ cup long-grain rice, uncooked
1⅔ cups chopped, cooked chicken (about ½ pound)
1 egg yolk
2 tablespoons fresh lemon juice
2 tablespoons chopped fresh dillweed
1 tablespoon chopped fresh chives
¼ teaspoon pepper

1. Heat oil in a saucepan over medium heat. Add onion and garlic; cook 3 minutes or until tender, stirring often. Add broth; bring to a boil. Stir in rice; cover, reduce heat, and simmer 20 minutes or until rice is tender. Stir in chicken. Bring just to a simmer; remove from heat.

2. Combine egg yolk and lemon juice; beat with a whisk until frothy. Stir about ½ cup hot broth mixture into egg mixture; stir egg mixture into broth mixture. Return saucepan to heat; cook over low heat until mixture reaches 160° (do not boil), stirring constantly. Stir in dillweed, chives, and pepper. Serve immediately. Yield: 4 (1-cup) servings.

NOTE: Avgolemono is a Greek soup that's made from chicken broth, egg yolk, lemon juice, and rice. Serve this main-dish soup with crusty French bread and a mixed greens salad.

Chicken Noodle Soup

2   teaspoons olive oil
¾   pound skinned, boned chicken breasts, cut into ½-inch
       pieces
1   cup chopped onion
1   clove garlic, minced
3   (14½-ounce) cans one-third-less salt chicken broth (such as
       Swanson's Natural Goodness)
⅔   cup diced carrot (about 2 medium)
½   teaspoon dried sage
¾   cup frozen English peas
4   ounces medium egg noodles, uncooked
½   teaspoon freshly ground pepper

1. Heat olive oil in a 4-quart saucepan over medium-high heat
1 minute. Add chicken, onion, and garlic. Cook 5 minutes or
until onion is golden, stirring often.

2. Add broth, carrot, and sage. Bring to a boil; cover, reduce heat,
and simmer 15 minutes or until chicken and carrot are tender.

3. Stir in peas, noodles, and pepper. Cook 5 minutes or until
peas and noodles are done. Yield: 8 (1-cup) servings.

 FOR A QUICK MEAL: Serve with whole wheat rolls and
low-fat strawberry ice cream.

POINTS:
2

EXCHANGES:
½ Starch
1½ Very Lean Meat

PER SERVING:
Calories 106
Carbohydrate 8.6g
Fat 1.9g (saturated 0.4g)
Fiber 1.4g
Protein 11.1g
Cholesterol 28mg
Sodium 411mg
Calcium 16mg
Iron 0.8mg

Manhattan Clam Chowder

POINTS:

2

EXCHANGES:

½ Starch

2 Vegetable

PER SERVING:

Calories 103

Carbohydrate 17.7g

Fat 1.2g (saturated 0.4g)

Fiber 1.7g

Protein 5.3g

Cholesterol 13mg

Sodium 594mg

Calcium 65mg

Iron 2.3mg

2   slices lower-sodium bacon, chopped
1⅓ cups finely chopped onion
½   cup diced celery
½   cup diced carrot
1   pound baking potatoes, peeled and diced
2   (15-ounce) cans stewed tomatoes, undrained
1   (14½-ounce) can one-third-less salt chicken broth (such as Swanson's Natural Goodness)
1   (8-ounce) bottle clam juice
1   teaspoon dried thyme
1   bay leaf
2   (6-ounce) cans minced clams, undrained
2   tablespoons chopped fresh parsley
¼   teaspoon pepper

1. Cook bacon in a 4-quart saucepan over medium-high heat until browned. Add onion, celery, and carrot; cook 4 minutes or until tender, stirring constantly. Stir in potato and next 5 ingredients; bring to a boil. Cover, reduce heat, and cook 30 minutes or until potato is tender.

2. Stir in clams, parsley, and pepper; bring to a boil. Reduce heat, and cook, uncovered, 3 minutes. Remove and discard bay leaf. Yield: 10 (1-cup) servings.

NOTE: Manhattan-style chowders such as this one are made with tomatoes rather than milk and cream like their New England-style counterparts.

side dishes

Warm Curried Fruit

POINTS:

2

EXCHANGES:

1½ Fruit

PER SERVING:

Calories 100
Carbohydrate 22.0g
Fat 1.4g (saturated 0.1g)
Fiber 2.0g
Protein 0.3g
Cholesterol 0mg
Sodium 107mg
Calcium 14mg
Iron 0.5mg

2 (15-ounce) cans peach halves in juice, drained
1 (15-ounce) can pear halves in juice, drained
1 (15.25-ounce) can pineapple chunks in juice, drained
1 (16.5-ounce) can pitted Royal Anne cherries in heavy
   syrup, drained
⅓ cup low-sugar orange marmalade
⅓ cup chutney
2 tablespoons reduced-calorie margarine
¾ teaspoon ground cinnamon
½ teaspoon curry powder

1. Combine fruit in a medium bowl.

2. Combine marmalade and remaining 4 ingredients in a small saucepan. Cook over medium heat until margarine melts, stirring often. Bring to a boil, stirring constantly; add to fruit, and toss gently.

3. Spoon fruit mixture into an 8-inch square baking dish. Cover and bake at 350° for 40 minutes or until mixture is bubbly. Yield: 11 (½-cup) servings.

 TIP: For more color, substitute Bing cherries for the Royal Anne cherries.

Green Bean Casserole

1 teaspoon vegetable oil

Cooking spray

½ cup chopped onion

½ cup chopped fresh mushrooms

2 (10-ounce) packages frozen French-style green beans, thawed and drained

1 (10¾-ounce) can reduced-fat, reduced-sodium cream of mushroom soup, undiluted

¼ cup fat-free milk

2 teaspoons low-sodium soy sauce

¼ teaspoon pepper

¼ cup crushed garlic-flavored croutons

POINTS:
1

EXCHANGES:
½ Starch
1 Vegetable
½ Fat

PER SERVING:
Calories 79
Carbohydrate 11.5g
Fat 2.5g (saturated 0.6g)
Fiber 2.1g
Protein 2.4g
Cholesterol 2mg
Sodium 281mg
Calcium 55mg
Iron 0.6mg

1. Heat oil in a large skillet coated with cooking spray; add onion and mushrooms. Cook 3 to 4 minutes or until onions are golden. Remove from heat, and stir in green beans.

2. Combine soup and next 3 ingredients, stirring with a whisk until smooth; add to green bean mixture. Stir well.

3. Spoon mixture into a 1½-quart baking dish coated with cooking spray. Bake, uncovered, at 375° for 25 minutes; sprinkle with crushed croutons. Bake 5 additional minutes or until bubbly. Yield: 6 (½-cup) servings.

FOR A QUICK MEAL: Serve with Country-Style Pork Chops (page 102).

Creamy Broccoli Casserole

POINTS:
1

EXCHANGES:
2 Vegetable
½ Fat

PER SERVING:
Calories 80
Carbohydrate 9.4g
Fat 2.8g (saturated 1.4g)
Fiber 2.3g
Protein 5.3g
Cholesterol 7mg
Sodium 304mg
Calcium 127mg
Iron 0.8mg

2   (10-ounce) packages frozen chopped broccoli
½   cup water
1   (10¾-ounce) can reduced-fat, reduced-sodium cream of
      mushroom soup, undiluted
1   (8-ounce) can sliced water chestnuts, drained
⅓   cup minced onion
¼   teaspoon salt
Cooking Spray
⅔   cup (2.6 ounces) shredded reduced-fat Cheddar cheese

1. Combine broccoli and water in a 1½-quart baking dish. Cover with heavy-duty plastic wrap and vent. Microwave at HIGH 7 to 9 minutes or until tender. Drain.

2. Combine broccoli, soup, and next 3 ingredients in a medium bowl; stir well. Spoon into a 1½-quart baking dish coated with cooking spray.

3. Cover and bake at 350° for 20 minutes or until bubbly. Uncover and sprinkle with cheese; bake 2 to 3 additional minutes or until cheese melts. Yield: 8 (½-cup) servings.

 COOKING SECRET: Drain the cooked broccoli well so the casserole won't have any excess liquid.

Italian Eggplant

Olive oil-flavored cooking spray
1   small eggplant, peeled and thinly sliced (about 1 pound)
Freshly ground pepper
1½ cups canned whole tomatoes, chopped
1   tablespoon minced onion
2   teaspoons dried basil
3   cloves garlic, minced
½   cup (2 ounces) shredded part-skim mozzarella cheese
1   tablespoon grated Parmesan cheese
2   tablespoons minced fresh parsley

1. Coat a jelly-roll pan with cooking spray. Arrange eggplant in pan in a single layer; coat with cooking spray. Broil 5½ inches from heat 6 to 7 minutes or until lightly browned. Turn and lightly coat with cooking spray; season with pepper. Broil 6 to 7 additional minutes or until lightly browned.

2. Combine tomatoes and next 3 ingredients in a small bowl.

3. Coat an 11- x 7-inch baking dish with cooking spray. Arrange eggplant in dish, and top with tomato mixture and mozzarella cheese. Bake, uncovered, at 375° for 12 to 15 minutes or until mozarella cheese melts.

4. Sprinkle Parmesan cheese and parsley over eggplant mixture. Serve immediately. Yield: 6 servings.

FOR A QUICK MEAL: Serve with Pasta Primavera (page 71) for a satisfying meatless meal.

POINTS:
1

EXCHANGES:
2 Vegetable
½ Fat

PER SERVING:
Calories 72
Carbohydrate 9.5g
Fat 2.4g (saturated 1.2g)
Fiber 2.2g
Protein 4.2g
Cholesterol 6mg
Sodium 215mg
Calcium 110mg
Iron 0.9mg

Braised Leek and Fennel Puree

POINTS:
2

EXCHANGES:
1 Starch
1 Vegetable

PER SERVING:
Calories 104
Carbohydrate 21.0g
Fat 0.8g (saturated 0.3g)
Fiber 1.5g
Protein 2.9g
Cholesterol 1mg
Sodium 305mg
Calcium 64mg
Iron 1.6mg

2   large leeks
2   large baking potatoes, peeled and quartered
1   medium fennel bulb, cut into eighths
Cooking spray
1   cup one-third-less salt chicken broth (such as Swanson's Natural Goodness)
½   cup dry white wine
3   tablespoons 66%-less-fat sour cream (such as Land O'Lakes)
1   tablespoon lemon juice
½   teaspoon salt
¼   teaspoon pepper

1. Remove root, tough outer leaves, and tops from leeks, leaving 2 inches of dark leaves. Wash thoroughly; cut into 2-inch pieces.

2. Cook potato in boiling water to cover 20 minutes or until tender; drain and mash with a potato masher. Set aside, and keep warm.

3. While potato cooks, place a large nonstick skillet over medium-high heat until hot. Add leeks and fennel, and coat with cooking spray. Cook 2 minutes, stirring constantly. Add chicken broth and wine. Bring to a boil; cover, reduce heat, and simmer 20 minutes. Uncover, increase heat to medium, and cook 10 additional minutes.

4. Process leek mixture, sour cream, and remaining 3 ingredients in food processor 30 seconds or until smooth. Add leek mixture to potato, stirring well. Yield 6 (½-cup) servings.

COOKING SECRET: Leeks are related to garlic and onions, but they are very mild. Wash leeks well, as they trap a good bit of dirt.

Spicy Black-Eyed Peas

2 slices lower-sodium bacon
1 (16-ounce) can whole tomatoes, undrained and chopped
1 (15.8-ounce) can black-eyed peas, rinsed and drained
2 cups frozen vegetable seasoning blend (such as McKenzie's)
1 teaspoon ground cumin
1 teaspoon dry mustard
½ teaspoon salt
½ teaspoon pepper
½ teaspoon curry powder
½ teaspoon chili powder
1 clove garlic, minced
2 tablespoons chopped fresh parsley

1. Cook bacon in a large skillet until crisp. Remove bacon; crumble and set aside. Drain skillet.

2. Combine tomatoes and next 9 ingredients in skillet. Bring to a boil; cover, reduce heat, and simmer 20 minutes, stirring occasionally. Spoon mixture into a serving dish; sprinkle with bacon and parsley. Yield: 6 (½-cup) servings.

 FOR A QUICK MEAL: Serve these spicy peas with Currant Glazed Pork Chops (page 103).

POINTS:
2

EXCHANGES:
1 Starch
½ Medium-Fat Meat

PER SERVING:
Calories 113
Carbohydrate 17.5g
Fat 2.2g (saturated 0.4g)
Fiber 3.5g
Protein 6.1g
Cholesterol 3mg
Sodium 586mg
Calcium 36mg
Iron 1.7mg

Cheese Fries (photo, cover)

POINTS:
3

EXCHANGES:
2 Starch

PER SERVING:
Calories 147
Carbohydrate 28.9g
Fat 1.7g (saturated 0.9g)
Fiber 2.1g
Protein 4.4g
Cholesterol 4mg
Sodium 190mg
Calcium 74mg
Iron 1.6mg

1½ pounds baking potatoes, unpeeled and cut into thin strips
    (about 3 potatoes)
Cooking spray
¼ cup grated Parmesan cheese
¼ teaspoon salt
¼ teaspoon pepper
¼ teaspoon paprika

1. Coat potato strips with cooking spray, and place in a large heavy-duty, zip-top plastic bag.

2. Combine cheese and remaining 3 ingredients; sprinkle over potato strips in bag. Seal bag and turn to coat potatoes well.

3. Arrange potato strips in a single layer on a large baking sheet or jelly-roll pan coated with cooking spray. Bake at 450° for 15 minutes, turning once. Serve immediately. Yield: 6 servings.

 FOR A QUICK MEAL: Serve with Classic Hamburgers (page 84), and for dessert, Chocolate Cream Pie (page 48).

Hearty Mashed Potatoes

3   large Yukon gold potatoes, peeled and cut into 1-inch cubes

3   slices lower-sodium bacon, chopped

4   cups thinly sliced green cabbage

½   cup one-third-less salt chicken broth (such as Swanson's Natural Goodness)

¼   cup fat-free milk

¼   cup 66%-less-fat sour cream (such as Land O'Lakes)

½   teaspoon salt

¼   teaspoon pepper

¼   cup sliced green onions

1. Cook potato in boiling water to cover 20 to 25 minutes or until tender. Drain well.

2. Meanwhile, cook bacon in a large skillet over medium heat 3 minutes or until browned. Add cabbage and chicken broth. Bring to a boil; cover, reduce heat, and simmer 10 minutes. Uncover, increase heat to high, and cook 2 additional minutes or until most of the liquid is absorbed.

3. Combine potato, milk, sour cream, salt, and pepper. Mash with a potato masher or beat at medium speed of an electric mixer until smooth. Add cabbage mixture and green onions; stir well. Yield: 8 (½-cup) servings.

TIP: Sliced cabbage and bits of bacon distinguish this delicious potato dish from traditional mashed potatoes.

POINTS:

3

EXCHANGES:

1½ Starch

½ Vegetable

½ Fat

PER SERVING:

Calories 160

Carbohydrate 26.3g

Fat 3.6g (saturated 1.5g)

Fiber 3.3g

Protein 6.0g

Cholesterol 8mg

Sodium 485mg

Calcium 87mg

Iron 1.3mg

Potatoes with Onions

POINTS:
1

EXCHANGE:
1 Starch

PER SERVING:
Calories 86
Carbohydrate 16.6g
Fat 1.3g (saturated 0.4g)
Fiber 1.7g
Protein 1.7g
Cholesterol 0mg
Sodium 284mg
Calcium 13mg
Iron 0.3mg

1 tablespoon reduced-calorie margarine
2 medium onions, sliced
3 medium Yukon gold potatoes, unpeeled and cut into
   1-inch cubes
1 (14½-ounce) can one-third-less salt chicken broth (such as
   Swanson's Natural Goodness)
½ teaspoon minced fresh thyme
¼ teaspoon salt
¼ teaspoon pepper

1. Melt margarine in a large skillet over medium heat; add onion, and cook 20 minutes or until golden, stirring often. Add potato and remaining ingredients; cover, reduce heat, and simmer 30 minutes. Uncover, increase heat to high, and simmer 3 to 5 additional minutes or until liquid is absorbed. Yield: 6 (½-cup) servings.

COOKING SECRET: Yukon gold potatoes give this dish a wonderful buttery flavor. Sprinkle ¼ cup shredded reduced-fat sharp Cheddar cheese over these potatoes for a delicious cheesy flavor option.

Dijon Scalloped Potatoes

¾ cup one-third-less salt chicken broth (such as Swanson's Natural Goodness)

½ cup sliced leeks

½ cup fat-free milk

2 tablespoons all-purpose flour

1 tablespoon Dijon mustard

¼ teaspoon dried dillweed

¼ teaspoon salt

⅛ to ¼ teaspoon pepper

4 cups peeled, thinly sliced baking potato (about 1½ pounds)

Cooking spray

POINTS:

2

EXCHANGES:

1½ Starch

PER SERVING:

Calories 116

Carbohydrate 25.0g

Fat 0.5g (saturated 0.1g)

Fiber 1.7g

Protein 2.9g

Cholesterol 0mg

Sodium 189mg

Calcium 37mg

Iron 0.6mg

1. Combine broth and leeks in a medium saucepan; bring to a boil. Cover, reduce heat, and simmer 5 minutes. Combine milk, and next 5 ingredients, stirring with a whisk until smooth. Add to broth mixture, stirring well. Cook 3 minutes or until mixture is thickened and bubbly, stirring constantly. Remove from heat.

2. Layer half of potato in a 1½-quart oval au gratin or baking dish coated with cooking spray; pour half of leek mixture over potato. Repeat layers with remaining potato and leek mixture. Cover and bake at 350° for 55 minutes. Uncover and bake 15 additional minutes or until potato is tender and lightly browned. Yield: 6 (⅔-cup) servings.

FOR A QUICK MEAL: Serve these potatoes with Steak au Poivre (page 92).

Candied Sweet Potatoes

POINTS:

4

EXCHANGES:

3½ Starch

1 Fat

PER SERVING:

Calories 239

Carbohydrate 49.5g

Fat 4.3g (saturated 1.6g)

Fiber 4.3g

Protein 2.4g

Cholesterol 7mg

Sodium 47mg

Calcium 47mg

Iron 1.3mg

2   large sweet potatoes (about 2½ pounds)

⅓   cup plus 1 tablespoon firmly packed brown sugar

½   teaspoon ground cinnamon

¼   teaspoon ground nutmeg

⅛   teaspoon ground allspice

½   cup unsweetened apple juice

2   tablespoons light butter (such as Land O'Lakes), melted

Cooking spray

2   tablespoons finely chopped pecans, toasted

1. Cook sweet potatoes in boiling water to cover 20 to 25 minutes or until tender. Drain; let cool to touch. Peel and cut into ½-inch slices.

2. Combine brown sugar and next 3 ingredients in a small saucepan; stir in apple juice and butter. Cook over medium heat 5 minutes, stirring occasionally.

3. Layer half of sweet potato slices in an 11- x 7-inch baking dish coated with cooking spray; drizzle with half of brown sugar mixture. Repeat layers. Sprinkle with pecans. Bake at 350° for 1 hour and 15 minutes or until bubbly, basting often with liquid in baking dish. Yield: 6 servings.

 COOKING SECRET: Frequently basting these sweet potatoes gives them a rich color and keeps them moist.

Sweet Potato Casserole

1 (14.5-ounce) can mashed sweet potatoes
2 tablespoons brown sugar
2 tablespoons fat-free milk
2 teaspoons reduced-calorie margarine, melted
¼ teaspoon salt
Cooking spray
¼ cup firmly packed brown sugar
2 tablespoons all-purpose flour
1 tablespoon reduced-calorie margarine
2 tablespoons chopped pecans

1. Combine first 5 ingredients in a bowl; stir well. Spoon sweet potato mixture into a 1-quart baking dish coated with cooking spray.

2. Combine ¼ cup brown sugar and flour; cut in margarine until mixture is crumbly. Stir in pecans; sprinkle pecan mixture over sweet potato mixture. Bake at 350° for 30 minutes or until thoroughly heated. Yield: 4 (½-cup) servings.

TIP: Canned mashed sweet potatoes are often labeled "yams." Look for them in the canned vegetable aisle of your supermarket.

POINTS:
5

EXCHANGES:
3 Starch
1 Fat

PER SERVING:
Calories 241
Carbohydrate 45.7g
Fat 6.0g (saturated 1.1g)
Fiber 2.2g
Protein 3.0g
Cholesterol 0mg
Sodium 281mg
Calcium 57mg
Iron 2.0mg

Yellow Squash Casserole (photo, page 158)

POINTS:
2

EXCHANGES:
2½ Vegetable
1 Fat

PER SERVING:
Calories 109
Carbohydrate 12.5g
Fat 4.6g (saturated 1.5g)
Fiber 3.1g
Protein 6.3g
Cholesterol 43mg
Sodium 241mg
Calcium 89mg
Iron 1.2mg

2 pounds yellow squash, sliced (about 6 cups)
1 cup finely chopped onion
1 teaspoon reduced-calorie margarine, melted
9 reduced-fat round buttery crackers, crushed and divided
¼ cup (1 ounce) shredded reduced-fat sharp Cheddar cheese
2 slices lower-sodium bacon, cooked and crumbled
1 (2-ounce) jar diced pimiento, drained
1 egg, lightly beaten
1 egg white
¼ teaspoon salt
¼ teaspoon pepper
Cooking spray

1. Combine squash and water to cover in a large Dutch oven; bring to a boil. Cover, reduce heat, and simmer 5 minutes or until squash is tender. Drain well, and mash; set aside.

2. Cook onion in margarine until tender. Combine onion, squash, ⅓ cup cracker crumbs, and next 7 ingredients. Spoon into a 2-quart baking dish coated with cooking spray. Sprinkle with remaining cracker crumbs. Bake, uncovered, at 350° for 45 minutes. Yield: 6 (½-cup) servings.

 COOKING SECRET: An equal amount of frozen squash, thawed, may be substituted for fresh squash.

Baked Tomatoes

Olive oil-flavored cooking spray
2 large tomatoes, cut into ½-inch-thick slices (10 slices)
⅓ cup sliced green onions
1½ teaspoons minced garlic
¾ teaspoon dried Italian seasoning
¼ teaspoon salt
¼ teaspoon pepper
¼ cup freshly grated Parmesan cheese

1. Coat a 13- x 9-inch baking dish with cooking spray. Arrange tomato slices in a single layer in dish.

2. Sprinkle green onions and remaining ingredients over tomato slices. Bake, uncovered, at 350° for 10 to 12 minutes or until thoroughly heated. Serve warm. Yield: 5 servings (2 slices per serving).

FOR A QUICK MEAL: Serve as a side dish to Fettuccine Alfredo (page 70).

POINTS:
1

EXCHANGE:
1 Vegetable

PER SERVING:
Calories 47
Carbohydrate 6.9g
Fat 1.6g (saturated 0.8g)
Fiber 1.6g
Protein 2.7g
Cholesterol 3mg
Sodium 193mg
Calcium 66mg
Iron 1.0mg

Turnip Greens with Canadian Bacon

POINTS:
1

EXCHANGES:
1½ Vegetable
½ Lean Meat

PER SERVING:
Calories 69
Carbohydrate 7.9g
Fat 2.0g (saturated 0.6g)
Fiber 2.9g
Protein 6.3g
Cholesterol 11mg
Sodium 819mg
Calcium 227mg
Iron 1.6mg

Olive oil-flavored cooking spray
1   (6-ounce) package Canadian bacon, cut into ½-inch pieces
2   (16-ounce) packages fresh turnip greens, coarsely chopped
¼   cup water
1   cup drained and chopped roasted red pepper
2   tablespoons balsamic vinegar
½   teaspoon salt
¼   teaspoon freshly ground pepper

1. Coat a large Dutch oven with cooking spray, and place over medium-high heat until hot. Add Canadian bacon and cook 3 to 4 minutes or until lightly browned. Add greens and water; bring to a boil. Cover, reduce heat to low, and cook 10 minutes or until greens are tender. Stir in red pepper and remaining ingredients. Cover, and simmer 3 additional minutes. Yield: 8 (½-cup) servings.

TIP: This is an easy way to prepare turnip greens that everyone will enjoy. The greens fill a large Dutch oven to the top, but they will cook down quickly.

Ratatouille

2 teaspoons olive oil
1 small onion, sliced
1 small eggplant, cut into ¾-inch cubes
1 (14-ounce) can stewed tomatoes, undrained
1 small yellow squash, cut in half lengthwise and thinly sliced
1 medium zucchini, cut in half lengthwise and thinly sliced
1 small green pepper, thinly sliced
4 cloves garlic, minced
1 teaspoon dried thyme
1 teaspoon dried basil
¼ teaspoon freshly ground pepper

1. Heat oil in a large nonstick skillet over medium heat until hot. Add onion and cook 5 minutes, or until tender, stirring constantly. Add eggplant; cook 5 additional minutes, stirring constantly.

2. Add stewed tomatoes and next 5 ingredients; stir well. Cover, reduce heat, and simmer 15 minutes or until vegetables are tender. Add basil and pepper; cook 2 additional minutes. Yield: 5 (1-cup) servings.

TIP: Serve on a bed of couscous or angel hair pasta as a side dish to grilled chicken or pork.

POINTS:
1

EXCHANGES:
3 Vegetable
½ Fat

PER SERVING:
Calories 85
Carbohydrate 15.4g
Fat 2.3g (saturated 0.3g)
Fiber 3.3g
Protein 2.7g
Cholesterol 0mg
Sodium 208mg
Calcium 60mg
Iron 1.6mg

Mushroom Risotto (photo, page 159)

POINTS:
3

EXCHANGES:
2 Starch

PER SERVING:
Calories 140
Carbohydrate 27.1g
Fat 1.5g (saturated 0.3g)
Fiber 0.8g
Protein 3.1g
Cholesterol 1mg
Sodium 315mg
Calcium 19mg
Iron 1.7mg

3 cups one-third-less salt chicken broth (such as Swanson's Natural Goodness)
2 teaspoons reduced-calorie margarine
½ teaspoon olive oil
1 small onion, finely chopped
½ (8-ounce) package sliced fresh mushrooms
¼ cup chopped green pepper
1¼ cups Arborio rice
½ cup dry white wine
2 tablespoons freshly grated Parmesan cheese
¼ teaspoon salt
⅛ teaspoon freshly ground pepper
Freshly shaved Parmesan cheese (optional)

1. Heat broth in a medium saucepan over low heat; keep warm.

2. Heat margarine and olive oil in a large saucepan over medium heat. Add onion, mushrooms, and green pepper. Cook, stirring constantly, 3 minutes or until vegetables are tender.

3. Add rice, stirring well. Add wine, and cook over medium-low heat, stirring constantly, until wine has been absorbed. Add enough hot broth to cover rice. Cook over medium heat, stirring constantly, until broth is absorbed. Continue adding broth 1 ladle at a time until broth is absorbed and rice is done, stirring constantly. (Add water as needed if rice is not done after all broth has been used.)

4. Stir in Parmesan cheese, salt, and pepper. Serve immediately. Garnish with freshly shaved Parmesan cheese, if desired. Yield: 8 (½-cup) servings.

 NOTE: Risotto is an Italian rice specialty that is worth the time required to stir the rice until it is delectably creamy.

Recipe Index

ACKNOWLEDGMENTS & CREDITS

Cyclamen Studio, Inc., Berkeley, CA

Christine's, Mountain Brook, AL

Fioriware, Zanesville, OH

Alice Goldsmith, New York, NY

Emile Henry USA Corp., Hazlet, NJ

Pastis & Co., New York, NY

Takashimaya, New York, NY

Woodbury's of Vermont, Burlington, VT

Sources of Nutrient Analysis Data:

Computrition, Inc., Chatsworth, CA, and
information provided by food manufacturers.

CONTRIBUTING PHOTOGRAPHERS

Billy Brown (pages 1, 3, 24, 43, 79, 118)

Mark Gooch (pages 4, 80, 100, 119, 140, 160)

CALORIE-BURNING ACTIVITIES

The numbers on this chart reflect how many calories are burned per minute by people of various weights during specific activities.

Activity	WEIGHT			
	120 lbs.	140 lbs.	160 lbs.	180 lbs.
	Calories burned per minute			
Basketball	7.5	8.8	10.0	11.3
Bowling	1.2	1.4	1.6	1.9
Cycling (10 m.p.h.)	5.5	6.4	7.3	8.2
Dancing (aerobic)	7.4	8.6	9.8	11.1
Dancing (social)	2.9	3.3	3.7	4.2
Gardening	5.0	5.9	6.7	7.5
Golf (power cart)	2.1	2.5	2.8	3.2
Golf (pull/carry clubs)	4.6	5.4	6.2	7.0
Hiking	4.5	5.2	6.0	6.7
Jogging	9.3	10.8	12.4	13.9
Running	11.4	13.2	15.1	17.0
Sitting quietly	1.2	1.3	1.5	1.7
Skating (ice and roller)	5.9	6.9	7.9	8.8
Skiing (cross-country)	7.5	8.8	10.0	11.3
Skiing (water and downhill)	5.7	6.6	7.6	8.5
Swimming (crawl, moderate pace)	7.8	9.0	10.3	11.6
Tennis	6.0	6.9	7.9	8.9
Walking (moderate pace)	6.5	7.6	8.7	9.7
Weight training	6.6	7.6	8.7	9.8

Reprinted with permission from the American Council on Exercise from *ACE Fit Facts*.